# LOOKING WITH FOREVER EYES

# Looking With Forever Eyes

*How to Live Now in the Light of Eternity*

## MARY WHELCHEL

SERVANT PUBLICATIONS
ANN ARBOR, MICHIGAN

Vine Books is an imprint of Servant Publications especially designed to serve evangelical Christians.

**Servant Publications—Mission Statement**
We are dedicated to publishing books that spread the gospel of Jesus Christ, help Christians to live in accordance with that gospel, promote renewal in the church, and bear witness to Christian unity.

Published by Servant Publications
P.O. Box 8617
Ann Arbor, Michigan 48107
www.servantpub.com

Cover design: UDG-DesignWorks, Sisters, Oreg.

03 04 05 06 10 9 8 7 6 5 4 3 2 1

Printed in the United States of America
ISBN 1-56955-290-8

*Library of Congress Cataloging-in-Publication Data*

Whelchel, Mary.
  Looking with forever eyes : how to live now in the light of eternity /
Mary Whelchel.
    p. cm.
Includes bibliographical references (p.        ).
  ISBN 1-56955-290-8
  1. Spiritual life--Christianity.  I. Title.
  BV4501.3 .W455 2003
  248.4--dc21
                                                2002152550

# Contents

# Introduction

# What Are *Forever* Eyes?

Little things bother me much more than big ones. I can stress out more over a late flight or a broken nail than I do over significant issues. Not because I think the little things are more important, but because I so easily lose my perspective on how truly unimportant they are.

Years ago I recognized that this was a major failing of my Type A, driven, controlling personality, and I knew I needed to change. But how? After all, I was born this way!

That's when God began to teach me some valuable lessons about polishing my personality so that it would become more Christlike. True, He made me "this way," but sin corrupted His creation in me, just as it has in all the universe. So, although I don't need to change my personality, I do need to allow His Spirit to smooth off the rough edges.

Recognizing this rough edge that needed some work, I asked God to help me find a way to overcome my tendency to overreact and lose my perspective so quickly and easily. Prayer became my first and most important weapon in this battle.

Then I heard of or read about a "gimmick" that has made a big difference to me in this struggle. It's a simple question I ask myself at those moments of diminutive-distress or trivial-trouble:

*What difference will this make in twenty-four hours?*

I determined that any incident that would not matter in twenty-four hours was truly not worthy of any negative reaction on my part. It was a foolish waste of my time and energy, and contributed too much unnecessary stress to my life. Furthermore, it almost always caused me to say and do things that were not wholesome, lovely, or a good testimony for an ambassador for Jesus Christ.

Therefore, I established a rule for myself: I am not allowed to expend any energy or emotion on anything that won't matter in twenty-four hours. That means I can't get angry or upset or frustrated about these things, because they truly are insignificant in the bigger scheme of things.

This simple technique has begun to bring my personality disorder under control. I have discovered that probably 80 percent of what upsets me at any given moment will not matter a whit in a short twenty-four hours. With one simple question, I have been able to lower my stress levels, control my propensity to overreact, and smooth those rough edges on my personality a bit.

The secret to this little trick is to force myself to have a longer perspective. As soon as I can get my eyes off the here and now and look ahead even a short twenty-four hours, my coping ability increases immensely. And all because I look at it from a long-term rather than a short-term perspective.

This simple illustration is what this book is all about: Learning to have a long-term perspective. However, we need more than a twenty-four-hour outlook. We need an eternal one. The apostle Paul reminded us of this when he wrote:

> *For our light and momentary troubles are achieving for us an eternal glory that far outweighs them all. So we fix our eyes not on what is seen, but on what is unseen. For what is seen is temporary, but what is unseen is eternal.*

2 CORINTHIANS 4:17-18

To analyze this statement from a strictly logical perspective, one would have to say that Paul was, at best, delusional, and at worst, stupid! To see what is unseen is a total contradiction in terms. Any first-grader can tell you that if you can't see something, there's no need trying to fix your eyes on it. It's unseeable!

Yet here we have the greatest Christian who ever lived, by most accounts, telling us to fix our eyes on what is unseen. Another paradox of Scripture that appears bewildering at first. Yet within the truth of this verse is a very straightforward, simple, and life-changing principle.

I call it "Looking with Forever Eyes," and it is indeed very simple, but it is not easy. It is the process of learning to live now in the light of eternity, and quite frankly, it is in opposition to our inborn, natural instincts.

Much of the Christian walk doesn't come naturally, I am discovering. Living by biblical principles has to be a God thing, something that He does in me. It's more than just being disciplined or hardworking or persistent. It has to begin with a motivation and a will on my part that is God-inspired and God-empowered.

"Motivation" and "will" are two key words that always determine success or failure. When I am properly motivated and absolutely determined to accomplish something, little can stand in my way. When my motivation is God-given and my will is God-empowered, I have what it takes to "do everything through him who gives me strength" (Phil 4:13b). Yet I have to relinquish my desires and my will to His control, and that's the hard part. It's what Jesus meant when He said:

> *For whoever wants to save his life will lose it, but whoever loses his life for me will save it.*
>
> LUKE 9:24

It takes Forever Eyes to understand this verse. Earthly eyes will never motivate you to lose your life for Jesus. Here-and-now eyes cannot see why or how losing your life for Jesus will save it. Yet with the ability and the will to look with Forever Eyes, to see what is unseen, we can see beyond the years of this earthly life and recognize the incredible blessing and joy that awaits us when we give up the control of our lives to Jesus Christ.

If I take that simple question I have used for many years to help me keep my cool and change a bit, I could ask:

*What difference will this make in eternity?*

Imagine the changes in my life—and yours—if we determined that we would regularly use that yardstick to determine and control our priorities, our time management, our relationships, and our dreams and aspirations. How much stress, frustration, anger, depression, and discouragement could we remove from our lives if we simply asked ourselves that question at least once a day?

**Who Has Forever Eyes?**

Taking a "long-term view" is not an exclusively Christian capability. People of many different religions, backgrounds, and motivations have learned the advantage of looking at consequences and effects beyond today's events. That's what strategic planning is all about in the business world, and no successful business can exist very long without looking beyond today's business conditions and preparing for what is coming.

There are many thoughtful people who carefully consider long-term effects in their own personal lives and make wise decisions and choices because of it. Even though we live in an age of instant gratification, there are still wise people around who have not succumbed to its deceptive lure, and we admire their ability to live with a long-term perspective.

However, looking with Forever Eyes is a cut above strategic planning or postponed gratification. It is living every part of our lives with a view of eternity, and that will control our priorities and our values. Furthermore, this view of eternity must be defined by God's Word, not by our own ideas of what is important in the light of eternity. The Forever Eyes of which I write are available only to those who have been born from above, born of the Spirit of God.

Jesus talked about this second birth when Nicodemus, a member of the Jewish ruling council, came to Him to find out who Jesus was. You'll find this very interesting encounter recorded in the Gospel of John, chapter three. Jesus said to Nicodemus, "I tell you the truth, no one can see the kingdom of God unless he is born again" (Jn 3:3b). The kingdom of God can be seen only with Forever Eyes, and Forever Eyes are our inheritance when we are born again.

As you begin this book, I would ask you to ask yourself this question: Have I been born again? Jesus went on to tell Nicodemus, "I tell you the truth, no one can enter the kingdom of God unless he is born of water and the Spirit" (Jn 3:5b). The right to enter the kingdom of God, to become a child of God, to see with Forever Eyes, is given to those—and only those—who have been born again.

To be born again is not difficult to do, but it takes faith and humility. You must humble yourself and admit that you are a sinner in need of a Savior. You must acknowledge that you have no power in yourself over your sinful nature, and you need to be forgiven and set free from the control of that sinful nature.

Then you must confirm that you are putting your trust in Jesus Christ, believing that He paid the price for your sins when He died on the cross, and you are accepting His free gift of eternal salvation. When you have done this with sincerity and according to God's Word, you are forgiven and you are born again. Second Corinthians 5:17 says, "Therefore, if anyone is in Christ, he is a new creation; the old has gone, the new has come!" This is what Jesus called being born again.

Like a newborn baby, you are born with new eyes—Forever Eyes. Your faith in Jesus Christ and the salvation He purchased for you through His death entitles you to Forever Eyes.

## Unused Forever Eyes

It must be noted, however, that there are far too many Christians who have indeed been born from above and have been given these new eyes, yet continue to live their everyday lives without ever using their Forever Eyes. Either they don't know they have them, they forget to use them, or they choose not to use them.

This is truly sad, because to miss seeing the unseen things is to miss much of the joy, excitement, and uniqueness of the Christian life. Think about it: If you had eyesight that allowed you to read a sign a mile off, to see for two miles with clarity, or to see beyond the horizon, wouldn't you feel very special? Nobody else around you would have such extraordinary eyesight, and that would give you an incredible advantage.

You could see trouble coming and avoid it. You could see good things up ahead and get there first. You would have more knowledge than those around you, more insight into what's ahead, less likelihood to misjudge or miscalculate.

Because of Forever Eyes, those of us born from above have even greater, more miraculous vision, and the advantages this offers us are phenomenal! We have the ability to:

- See consequences
- Avoid temptation
- Establish correct priorities
- Make the best use of our time
- Love unlovable people
- Avoid the tyranny of the urgent
- Discern people and their intentions more clearly
- Accept the uncontrollable
- Live a contented life

This is not an exhaustive list. There are more advantages to this type of a perspective than my mind can conceive, and these are all ours when we choose to look at life through Forever Eyes.

So, if you've got a set of these Forever Eyes, why not use them? Can you think of a good reason not to? Beats me. As I've begun to write this book that has been on my heart for many years, I've prayed that God will write it into my heart in a new way. To have this ability and not take advantage of it is foolishness at best, and disaster at worst.

*What difference will this make in eternity?* I hope that by the time you finish reading this book that question will be emblazoned in your memory, and you will be inspired and challenged to number your days and live now in the light of eternity. You'll never be sorry you did.

# One

# Looking at God With *Forever* Eyes

We often talk and sing about seeing God, or wanting to see God, or looking forward to seeing God. Job declared:

> *I know that my Redeemer lives, and that in the end he will stand upon the earth. And after my skin has been destroyed, yet in my flesh I will see God; I myself will see him with my own eyes—I, and not another. How my heart yearns within me!*
>
> JOB 19:25-27

We all share his yearning to see God. Can you imagine seeing God? One glimpse would take your breath away, blinding you. It would be more than earthly eyes could handle.

Yet how many times have you thought that if you could see God a little better, see some evidence of His existence, some proof of His love, some confirmation of His protection, then you could have faith? Then you could face the unknown. Then you could handle life. If only you could see God.

The disciples had the same feelings. Jesus told them,

> *I am the way and the truth and the life. No one comes to the Father except through me. If you really knew me, you would know my Father as well. From now on, you do know him and have seen him.*
>
> JOHN 14:6-7

Philip reacted as I would have, I think. He heard what Jesus said—that they had already seen God—so he figured he had missed it somehow. I can hear his mental wheels turning: *We have seen the Father? When? Where?* So, he made the obvious request:

> *Philip said, "Lord, show us the Father and that will be enough for us."*
> JOHN 14:8

I can fully relate to Philip's request. It would be enough for me. Can't you hear his heart pacing faster as he imagines seeing the Father? I think this was a childlike response on Philip's part, not a sarcastic challenge. I think he was sincere when he said, "Lord, show us the Father," and he was hoping for just that. All his doubts, all his fears, all his questions, all his worries would be forever resolved with one look at the Father. *Show us the Father, and that's enough!*

> *Jesus answered, "Don't you know me, Philip, even after I have been among you such a long time? Anyone who has seen me has seen the Father. How can you say, 'Show us the Father'?"*
> JOHN 14:9

## Look at Jesus

Jesus was astonished at Philip's inability to recognize that he had been seeing the Father all along because he had been seeing Jesus. He must have been dumbfounded at His follower's blindness. "Anyone who has seen me has seen the Father," He said. How could Philip have missed it?

Like Philip, we often miss seeing the Father because we're not looking at the Son. The writer to the Hebrews tells us that "The Son is the radiance of God's glory and the exact representation of his being, sustaining all things by his powerful word" (Heb 1:3a).

John wrote: "No one has ever seen God, but God the One and Only, who is at the Father's side, has made him known" (Jn 1:18).

The One at the Father's side is Jesus, and we can see God because we can see Jesus. Someday we'll see Jesus face to face in His glorified body. Someday our faith will turn to sight and we shall behold Him. Just thinking about that makes my heart beat faster.

Yet for the here and now, we see Jesus by looking with Forever Eyes. The writer to the Hebrews admonishes us:

*Let us fix our eyes on Jesus, the author and perfecter of our faith, who for the joy set before him endured the cross, scorning its shame, and sat down at the right hand of the throne of God.*

HEBREWS 12:2

This must become our daily prayer, if we would see God: that our eyes will stay fixed on Jesus. This, of course, requires Forever Eyes, eyes that are unique, because we can't see Jesus in the flesh yet. The disciples had that advantage over us; they saw the man Jesus. We haven't yet, though we know we will see him one day face-to-face in our flesh, as Job reminds us.

Since I'm a "how-to" person, my next question is "How do I see God by seeing Jesus, since I can't even see Jesus now? What does that look like in everyday living?" Here are some thoughts that have been helpful to me.

### Get to Know Jesus

Jesus said, "Now this is eternal life: that they may know you, the only true God, and Jesus Christ, whom you have sent" (Jn 17:3). How do we get to know someone? By spending time with that person; by sharing our life with that person; by making that person a high priority in our life. The same is true in getting to know Jesus.

Of course, we must get to know Jesus through the Bible, specifically through the four Gospels. I strongly recommend that you read through the Gospels continuously. Every day, read at least a chapter in one of the Gospels. I start in Matthew, read through Mark, Luke, and John, and then start over again in Matthew.

It has been very helpful to me, as I read a Gospel chapter each day, to discipline myself to read that chapter with fresh eyes. I try to read it as though I've never read it before. Those of us who have heard the Gospel stories many times, who have read these chapters before, can become immune to the incredible awesomeness of Jesus Christ. We can miss so much.

If I find my mind wandering, or I'm just letting the words fly by without really focusing on what I'm reading, I make myself start the chapter over again. If you have a short attention span, like I do, you may also find this to be a necessary discipline.

Another helpful discipline in reading the Gospels is to put yourself in the action. I try to imagine that I'm one of the disciples present in that Gospel chapter. For example, imagine that you are Peter when the Lord tells His disciples that He wants them to understand that He must die. Peter rebukes the Lord and insists that this cannot happen to Jesus. However, Jesus stuns Peter with his refusal to accept his rebuke. "Get behind me, Satan! You are a stumbling block to me; you do not have in mind the things of God, but the things of men" (Mt 16:23b).

Can you put yourself in Peter's shoes? He surely thinks he is being very spiritual and very caring in telling the Lord that He must not die. Peter expects the Lord to appreciate his rebuke. Doesn't it show how much Peter cares about Jesus? Instead, Peter is thrown back on his heels by a sharp reprimand from the Lord.

If you put yourself in Peter's shoes, you will think in much more depth about what Jesus has just said. You will gain much more insight into the radical truth that Jesus is preaching and how difficult it was for the disciples to understand Him. You will get to know Jesus much better.

So, read about Jesus with Forever Eyes and with a prayer that God will open your eyes to understanding and help you to truly get to know Jesus.

## Magnify the Lord

Because we don't have perfect eyesight and can't see everything, we have learned to magnify things. It's a common practice. We can magnify things by actually enlarging them, as with photos and on our copiers. Or we can magnify something by making it appear larger, as we do with magnifying glasses.

David spoke of magnifying the Lord:

Psalm 34:3 (KJV): "O magnify the Lord with me, and let us exalt his name together."
Psalm 35:27b (KJV): "Let them say continually, 'Let the Lord be magnified, which hath pleasure in the prosperity of his servant.'"
Psalm 40:16 (KJV): "Let all those that seek thee rejoice and be glad in thee: let such as love thy salvation say continually, 'The Lord be magnified.'"

What does it mean to magnify the Lord? Have you ever been to a concert or a play where your seats in the theater were so far back that the people on stage looked like they were two inches tall? That's why people bring opera glasses—magnifying glasses—to the theater with them. They use those glasses to magnify the people on stage, so they can see them better, even from a long distance away. These magical glasses make those people on stage increase in size. Instantly they grow to ten times the size they were before, or maybe even more.

Think of how a magnifying glass works. The object on which it is focused does not increase in size. Rather, the magnifying glass changes our eyesight and allows us to see the object closer to its true-life size.

In a theater, we use opera glasses to have a better view of the actors and actresses on stage. If you were right up there on stage with them, you would not need the glasses, for you would see them exactly as they are. Since your seats are so far away, however, the magnifying glasses allow you to see the actors and actresses better, more life-size, more like they really are.

The problem is not that the people on stage are too small; the problem is that you are too far away from them. It does not benefit them to be magnified. The magnification is done for your benefit.

That's a little of what it means to magnify the Lord. We just aren't in a position yet to see Him as clearly as we need to see Him. Our minds are too small, our experience is too limited, and our seats are too far away.

In 1 Corinthians 13:12 we read, "Now we see but a poor reflection as in a mirror; then we shall see face to face." We know that someday we'll be up there on stage with Jesus, and we won't have any difficulty at all seeing Him as He is. Yet until that time, we need our magnifying glasses. Jesus doesn't need to be larger; we need to see Him in a form closer to His true image.

## How to Magnify the Lord

Thus, while here on this earth, we need to magnify the Lord in our minds—by looking at Him with Forever Eyes. How do we do that?

You magnify the Lord when you think about Him a great deal. You think about Him a great deal when you spend time in daily conversation with Him and daily Bible reading.

You magnify the Lord when you worship Him, privately and together with other believers. Did you notice that Psalm 34:3 said to magnify the Lord *with me,* and told us to exalt his name *together?* When we meet together to sing and praise God, we not only magnify Him in our own minds but we also help and encourage others to do the same.

You know, this doesn't have to be done in a formal worship service. Any time we are together with believers, we should try to focus our conversations on Jesus. I once heard someone quote a great preacher who had made a commitment to the Lord early in his life. He told the Lord that whenever he had the opportunity to determine the direction of a conversation, he would try to turn the conversation toward Jesus.

Just think about that. What if we had that kind of commitment today? If we turn more and more of our conversations toward Jesus, He will be magnified in our minds. We need to do that for ourselves and for each other.

You magnify the Lord when you refuse to allow the wrong things to be magnified in your mind. For example, in the midst of your day when someone says something hurtful to you or does something to make you angry, instead of thinking about that negative thing, start magnifying the Lord in your mind. Force yourself to think about the goodness of God. Instead of magnifying the hurt or the frustration, stop and magnify the Lord instead.

You magnify the Lord when you intentionally take your mind off of yourself and put it on the Lord. Not long ago, I spent a couple of miserable months magnifying myself. I drove myself into discouragement, into a major pity party, into a rotten attitude toward others, into a critical spirit, into a desire to quit! I tried to keep it under cover— after all, Christian leaders shouldn't allow such things to happen, right? Yet it showed, and I was miserable, and I managed to spread the misery to those around me, I'm sure.

In dragging myself out of this depressed state, what I instantly recognized and confessed was that I had magnified my problems and my circumstances way out of proportion to reality, because I had thought about me far more than I had thought about the Lord! And I've even written a book (*What Would Jesus Think?*) on bringing your thought life into captivity!

### Adjust Your Focus

A few years ago I was talking with a friend who has to deal with a painful past. There was some mental and physical abuse in her childhood, and she has struggled with the aftereffects. Yet she was sharing with me how God is healing her and giving her freedom from this painful past.

"Mary," she said to me, "I finally came to the conclusion that I could either magnify my past or magnify my Lord. If I magnify the past, I'll be defeated and depressed forever. So I've chosen to magnify the Lord in my life."

It's very easy to magnify the wrong thing. You see, when I'm holding those opera glasses at the theater, I choose where I want to focus them. I can look at the star on stage, or I can look at the people in the front row. I can look at the important things that are happening, or I can instead watch the trivial, unimportant things. So, what I see in those magnifying glasses depends on which way I turn them and where I focus them.

The same is true with what is magnified in our minds. It depends on our focus. If I choose to set my sights on the wrong things, and they become magnified, then I find myself in lots of mental and emotional upheaval. My job, therefore, is to keep those magnifying glasses focused on the good things, on the Lord.

That's what my friend has done; she has made a decision to focus her magnifying glasses on Jesus rather than on her past. Every time her mind wants to go back to those things of the past that keep her mired down in pain, she simply stops and refocuses on Jesus.

Make sure, whatever you do, that each day you focus your magnifying glasses on Jesus at the beginning of your day, and that you keep them there all day long. You can think of it as taking your opera glasses with you all day, after you have focused them on Jesus at the beginning of the day.

Start each day by praying, "Lord, by Your grace, I'm going to keep my eyes on You today, regardless of the activity all around me, or the many things I have to do. Even though there are problems and hurts to distract me, I'm going to see You, magnified and glorified. I choose to magnify You today, Lord."

"Let us fix our eyes on Jesus," Hebrews 12:2 begins. Notice that the responsibility for where we fix our eyes lies with us. Let *us* fix our eyes.... We decide whether we will look with Forever Eyes and magnify the Lord, or whether we will continue to be limited to earthly eyes.

Keep your eyes fixed on Jesus—that's what it means to magnify the Lord.

Will you make a commitment today to magnify the Lord? When

you make that commitment, it will start to crowd out all the negative things, and you'll discover that life is sweeter, Jesus is nearer, and you have a little taste of what it's going to be like in heaven, when you'll be right up front and see Jesus face to face.

## Two

# Looking at Myself and My Past With *Forever* Eyes

One of the shocking realizations that comes with age and maturity is that we see ourselves very differently than other people see us. This is not only shocking but also frightening, and therefore many people never allow themselves to think in those terms. Our own self-images are strongly embedded in our minds and to see ourselves in a different way or to realize that others see us very differently is disturbing and worrisome.

I remember years ago a fairly good friend telling me that she would love to invite me over for dinner sometime, but she knew how busy I was and she knew that I was never lonely. Never lonely! Whatever gave her that idea? I was a single mom, struggling with my identity and my place in a society built for two. Yet she saw me as totally self-sufficient and never needing fellowship or help. How did she get that picture of me?

I've come to learn that lots of people see me that way. It must be the image I portray, but it is not how I see myself. I know the butterflies that swim in my stomach with regularity, the insecurities that plague my self-image, the distorted reflections I see in my mirror. I know how quickly and frequently I see myself through the prism of my past, of my accomplishments and failures, of my possessions and status. I know how I am prone to measure myself in comparison with others, how much I base my self-worth and significance on that infamous ladder of success and which rung I'm on at the moment.

If seeing myself as others see me is challenging, seeing myself as God sees me is more so. It definitely requires Forever Eyes. I must first of all know how God sees me and then I must intentionally set my mind on that knowledge. Perhaps it would help to think about how God sees us.

## We Are God's Intentional Creation

My good friend Lucille has gone on ahead of me to be with the Lord. I'll never forget how she came to saving faith in the Lord Jesus Christ. Through friendships in our church, she began attending our women's events and church services. The gospel had never really been explained to her, though she had faithfully attended her church most of her life. Despite her religious upbringing, she didn't know that God loved her and had created her for Himself.

After coming to that knowledge and becoming a new creation in Christ Jesus, she told me that for all of her life, as the youngest of several children, her mother had told her that she had been a mistake. Her birth had not been planned, and as a result, her presence in the family had caused great inconvenience and hardship. Not recognizing the harm that her words were inflicting, Lucille's mother had constantly reminded her that she was a mistake.

As a result, Lucille spent all of her life trying to be the perfect child, so that her mother would recognize her significance. If she could earn her mother's approval, she felt, then she would not be a mistake.

Coming to know Jesus and understanding that she was God's intentional creation was a tremendous revelation for Lucille. For the few years she knew the Lord before her death, she simply glowed in the knowledge that God loved her and she was not a mistake. You could see it in her face, even when she was facing death from cancer. There was no fear, and never again was there any doubt that the God of all creation held her in the palm of His hand, for she was His daughter.

In Colossians 1:16 we read:

*For by him [Jesus Christ] all things were created: things in heaven and on earth, visible and invisible, whether thrones or powers or rulers or authorities; all things were created by him and for him.*

Since you are on earth and you are visible, you can be certain that you, too, were created by Him. Yet consider the last two words in that verse: you were created *for Him!* Not just by Him, but for Him! To create is to cause something unique to come into being. A creation is something that comes from a person's own thoughts or imagination, like a work of art or an invention. When you create something like that, it belongs to you.

The depth of this truth is life changing. The Almighty God created you and me, and we were created for Him—for His purposes, for His reasons. That knowledge alone brings significance into our lives.

## We Were Created for His Pleasure

Remember the wonderful movie *Chariots of Fire,* the story of that remarkable Olympic champion, the Scottish runner, Eric Liddel, who was a strong Christian committed to Jesus Christ? His missionary sister is portrayed as being concerned about his running career because she felt he was neglecting his calling and not putting God first. Yet Eric said to his sister, "Oh, don't you see, Jenny? God made me fast. And when I run, I feel His pleasure."

Revelation 4:11 (KJV) puts it this way:

*Thou art worthy, O Lord, to receive glory and honor and power: for thou hast created all things, and for thy pleasure they are and were created.*

We were created for His pleasure. This is an idea that many of us have never really considered or believed, for it is mind-boggling to think that the God of all the universe would find pleasure in us. Yet remember—He has created us, and we are His works of art. He created us because He wanted to, and we bring Him pleasure simply because we are His creation.

When I try to comprehend that I give God pleasure, I immediately focus on all the things I've done wrong that have brought Him anything but pleasure. I remember the broken promises, the unloving ways, the years of rebellion, my selfish motivation even to this day. I shake my head and say, "How could I bring God pleasure? I'm so imperfect!"

What you and I must constantly make ourselves remember, however, is that we bring God pleasure because He created us, not because we perform well. While it is true that we can grieve His heart by not allowing Him to live His life through us, it is still true that we are created for His pleasure, and that never changes.

J.I. Packer puts this so well in his wonderful classic, *Knowing God:*

There is tremendous relief in knowing that His love to me is utterly realistic, based at every point on prior knowledge of the worst about me, so that no discovery now can disillusion Him about me, in the way I am so often disillusioned about myself, and quench His determination to bless me ... for some unfathomable reason, He wants me as His friend, and desires to be my friend....[1]

It is unfathomable, but it is nonetheless true: God takes pleasure in you. Eric Liddel's faith was strong enough and simple enough to realize that because God made him fast, his speed brought God pleasure. Can you say that about yourself? You should be able to verbalize how God has created you to bring Him pleasure. Maybe you could say: "Because God made me a good listener, I bring God pleasure when I listen and care about others." Or, "Because God made me a good organizer, I bring God pleasure when I organize events and run them smoothly." Or, "Because God made me a speaker, I bring God pleasure when I give a good talk or make a good presentation."

It really doesn't matter how God has created us; we are all very different in our gifts and abilities. Yet we were all created for His pleasure. It is not pride on our part to recognize how God has created us. Eric Liddel gave God the credit for his fast body, but he also recognized that it was a gift from God to bring God pleasure.

### Worthy Because We Are Loved

In his book *Reaching for the Invisible God*, Philip Yancey quotes from a sermon he heard by Ian Pitt-Watson: "Some things are loved because they are worthy; some things are worthy because they are loved."[2]

We are worthy because we are loved by the eternal God. When we can see ourselves through Forever Eyes and not only acknowledge in our heads but rejoice in our hearts that God loves us just because He loves us, it begins to change the way we see ourselves.

I want to encourage you to realize that God delights in you. I love this verse from Zephaniah 3:17:

*The Lord your God is with you,*
*he is mighty to save.*

*He will take great delight in you,*
*he will quiet you with his love,*
*he will rejoice over you with singing.*

Don't you love that imagery of God rejoicing over you with singing? We often rejoice and take delight in God through singing, but to think that He does the same over us is an amazing thought. That makes it a lot easier to get out of bed in the morning and find purpose in life.

## We Were Created for His Glory

Isaiah 43 is a wonderful chapter of encouragement, and if you haven't read it lately, I hope you will. Here are a few verses from that chapter:

*But now, this is what the Lord says—he who created you, O Jacob, he who formed you, O Israel: "Fear not, for I have redeemed you; I have summoned you by name; you are mine. When you pass through the waters, I will be with you; and when you pass through the rivers, they will not sweep over you. When you walk through the fire, you will not be burned; the flames will not set you ablaze. For I am the Lord, your God, the Holy one of Israel, your Savior; I give Egypt for your ransom, Cush and Seba in your stead. Since you are precious and honored in my sight, and because I love you, I will give men in exchange for you, and people in exchange for your life.*

ISAIAH 43:1-4

*Bring my sons from afar and my daughters from the ends of the earth—everyone who is called by my name, whom I created for my glory, whom I formed and made.*

ISAIAH 43:6b-7

God created you, you are His, He called you by name, you are precious to Him, He loves you—and you were created *for His glory.* Is that how you see yourself? If not, you haven't been looking with Forever Eyes.

When great artists paint their masterpieces, we admire the paintings because of their beauty and creativity. Yet who gets the glory for the painting? The artist, of course. The painting did not paint itself; we don't say, "Thank you, masterpiece, for creating this beautiful picture for us." No, we say, "This artist is wonderful; this artist is great." The masterpiece brings glory to the artist.

Because the Master created you, you are meant to bring glory to Him. The very fact that you have been created shows His power and wonder. God knit you together in your mother's womb and you are fearfully and wonderfully made (see Ps 139:13-14).

## Looking Through the Eyes of Your Past

There are many Christians who know these facts but never live in their freedom. They continue to see themselves through the eyes of their past. Remembering all the mistakes and the mess that is in their history book, they assume that God sees them the same way they see themselves, since God knows all about their past. It's understandable, since the world system works that way.

If you've ever applied for a loan or a mortgage, you know that one of the determining factors is your past credit record. One small slipup even years ago can disqualify you for that loan. Try to convince a college registrar that those poor grades from your past do not reflect who you are now. Those grades are on that transcript forever, condemning you for past failures.

The people in our lives are often equally unforgiving. Throwing our past mistakes in our faces seems to be one of their favorite pastimes. Will they never let us off the hook?

I think of a woman I know who has been confronted with a husband's adulterous relationship. Though her spouse has promised it will never happen again, she tells me that every time she looks at her husband she sees him with the other woman. The past is so painful and so repulsive that it will take God's grace poured out in buckets to ever see him again without the "A" word emblazoned on his forehead.

If people see us through the filter of our pasts, and we see ourselves that way as well, how could God not also be forever influenced and biased by our past, especially since He knows the worst about us? Our human brains don't comprehend this easily. It truly takes Forever Eyes to even begin to live in the freedom brought by the knowledge that God does not condemn us with our past, once we repent of it and confess it. Bask in these wonderful truths from Psalm 103:

> *[The Lord] does not treat us as our sins deserve or repay us according to our iniquities. For as high as the heavens are above the earth, so great is his love for those who fear him; as far as the east is from the west, so far has he removed our transgressions from us. As a father has compassion on his children, so the Lord has compassion on those who fear him; for he knows how we are formed, he remembers that we are dust.*
>
> PSALM 103:10-14

To His wayward and disobedient Israel, He said:

*I, even I, am he who blots out your transgressions, for my own sake,
and remembers your sins no more.*

ISAIAH 43:25

The apostle Paul reminds us that:

*Therefore, there is now no condemnation for those who are in Christ
Jesus, because through Christ Jesus the law of the Spirit of life set me
free from the law of sin and death.*

ROMANS 8:1-2

I love the verse from one of the songs my friend Damaris Carbaugh
sings so beautifully:

Do you know what it's like for God to be your friend,
To talk to Him with nothing in between?
Do you know what it's like when the day comes to an end,
To sleep in peace because your heart is clean?
Do you know what it's like when the accuser comes your way?
To look him squarely in the eye with confidence and say:
He has forgiven me,
My sin has been washed from His memory,
By the blood of the Lamb of Calvary
He has forgiven me.*

* "He Has Forgiven Me"—words and music by Marie Armenia© 1995, Penny Hill
Publishing, P.O. Box 257, Franklin, TN 37065. Used by permission. All rights reserved.

To live with the monkey of our past on our backs is to miss the freedom that Jesus died to give us. Our sins have been washed from His memory, and if He has forgiven us, who are we to not forgive ourselves? If God looks at us and sees us as righteous in His sight because of Jesus, what arrogance and foolishness on our part to keep seeing ourselves through the lens of our past.

The enemy of your soul will mire you down with your past if you allow him to. It's one of his favorite tactics to keep you from joy, peace, and effectiveness. Pray daily that you will see yourself through God's eyes, Forever Eyes, and live now in the light of how God sees you.

I have often said that God chose to use me as a dramatic demonstration of His incredible power and His astonishing grace. Of all people, I don't deserve to be His instrument of love and grace. I rebelled against Him for ten long years, and I deserve to have to live with those consequences through the rest of my days. Yet God decided to show how powerful and how forgiving He is, and He continues to allow me the privilege of serving Him.

You see, the less He has to work with, the more God gets the glory for the workmanship! He is capable of taking a desert and turning it into a garden. He is masterful at taking ashes and turning them into beauty. He is incredible at transforming ruined lives into testimonies of His greatness. Here's a wonderful passage from Isaiah 61:3b:

> *To bestow on them a crown of beauty instead of ashes, the oil of gladness instead of mourning, and a garment of praise instead of a spirit of despair. They will be called oaks of righteousness, a planting of the Lord for the display of his splendor.*

No longer are we saddled with the names from our past. No longer are we called "backslider" or "cheater" or "adulterer" or "liar" or "faithless one." Our name is now "an oak of righteousness," because we have been given the righteousness of Jesus Christ.

Philippians 3:9 tells us that we have a righteousness now that comes through faith in Christ, not a righteousness of our own. That is good news, because our own righteousness is like filthy rags to God. So, through God's eyes we are "in Christ" and He sees us clothed in the righteousness of Jesus—forgiven and clean.

## We Are Heirs of God and Co-Heirs With Christ

Romans 8:17 tells us, "Now if we are children, then we are heirs—heirs of God and co-heirs with Christ, if indeed we share in his sufferings in order that we may also share in his glory." If we are heirs of God, that means we're in line to inherit God's riches. If we are co-heirs with Christ, that means we'll inherit the Father's great riches equally with Christ.

When you look at yourself, do you see an heir? How often do you remind yourself that you are slated to inherit all of God's riches, co-equally with Jesus Himself? That's how God sees you, because that's the truth of who you are when you are His child. Have you looked with Forever Eyes and seen your "heirship" lately?

When you focus on who you are in Christ and His power in you, then you can have victory over the old self-images and inadequacies and the way you've seen yourself all these years. You can truly learn to see yourself and your past with Forever Eyes.

## You Have a Standing Invitation to God's Throne Room

Years ago I began to see myself with Forever Eyes by seeing myself going into God's throne room in prayer. It truly began to revolutionize my understanding of how God sees me. A good friend encouraged me to share this imagery with others, and reluctantly I began to do so. I suppose God has used this as much or more than any other message I've given to encourage others to see themselves as God sees them.

I'm not certain this will translate on paper as well as it does in a dramatic setting, but hoping that it will help you to see yourself with Forever Eyes, I'm going to include it here.

You will have to use your imagination, but it is all based on scriptural truths. I've imagined the setting, but I have not distorted the truth of the Bible. Please do understand, however, that this conversation is not recorded anywhere in Scripture, nor are we told there is such a "head angel" as I have here imagined. I'm simply trying to use word pictures to help you understand truth in a new way.

First, picture a room of grandeur and opulence never imagined on this earth. Hollywood could never touch it. This room is absolutely gigantic, and as you enter, your eyes just cannot begin to take it all in. Everywhere you look there are emeralds, pearls, diamonds—every type of jewel imaginable. The floor is made of pure gold, gleaming and glorious. The room is so bright it almost blinds you.

In the center of this huge room is a throne that simply defies description. Mere words could never do it justice. It is huge and impressive beyond belief. A rainbow resembling an emerald encircles the throne, and in front of the throne is a sea of crystal (see Rv 4:3, 6).

Around this throne are untold numbers of angels, praising and guarding the One who sits on the throne, God the Creator. These are angels of such beauty and magnificence that they are indescribable.

They are huge, with wingspans beyond belief, and their garments shine with a dazzling light. These angels sing forever in this room—songs you've never heard before, more glorious than any sound you could possibly imagine. They sing songs of praise to God who sits on the throne.

Now, you must picture me entering this throne room. As I come into the room, my appearance is in stark contrast to all around. I look like a scruffy kid, without any glory or beauty. I'm so insignificant in comparison to everything else in this incredible room that I could easily be trampled on without notice. However, I am dressed in a beautiful, magnificent robe.

As I enter, someone notices me. It's the head angel, the one in charge of keeping everything just perfect. He walks up to me and says,

*Angel:* Excuse me, but who are you? I think you must be lost—surely you're not planning to enter our throne room.

*Mary:* Well, I know that I appear very insignificant and a bit out of place compared to everyone else, but yes, I was planning to enter.

*Angel:* How can you be so brazen? What are you going to do in the throne room?

*Mary:* Well, you see, I plan to go right up to the throne and talk to God.

*Angel:* Oh, my, that would be funny if it were not so arrogant on your part. You're planning to go directly up to the throne and talk to God? My dear, look at you. Do you think God wants to talk to you? He's very busy you know—and there are many more important things on His agenda today.

*Mary:* Oh, sir, I realize that, and I know that it seems entirely inappropriate for me to approach His throne, but you see, He has given me a personal invitation. As a matter of fact, He has said that I may come into His presence any time I wish, and—you really will have a hard time believing this—He has said that I may approach His throne with boldness (see Heb 4:16).

*Angel:* With boldness? But look at you. You're not worthy of being in His presence. Do you see all these angels here—they wouldn't just walk up to His throne with boldness.

*Mary:* I know, sir, but you see, I'm not an angel. I'm His child.

*Angel:* His child?

*Mary:* Yes, isn't that incredible? I'm His child. I would have been satisfied just to worship Him from afar, but He has told me that since I have accepted His Son as my Savior, I'm no longer an alien. I am now His child (see Eph 2:19). He has told me that I can call Him Father.

*Angel:* Father? Can this be true? You would call God, the Creator of the entire universe, whom the angels worship in fear and splendor— you would dare to call Him Father?

*Mary:* I recognize how difficult it is to believe that, sir. Frankly, I find it a continual source of amazement myself that He would allow me to call Him Father. Yet not only can I call Him Father, He has told me I may call Him "Abba Father"—dearest Father, Daddy (see Rom 8:15).

*Angel:* Do you realize how incredible this all is, my dear child? I just can't imagine why He would allow you such privileges—you, of all people.

*Mary:* Well, sir, let me tell you, it's not because of anything I've done that has made me worthy. As you can see, I'm not very pretty and I have no credits to my account that would make me presentable to God. Except for one—I have accepted His Son as my Savior, and when I did that, He gave me this gorgeous robe to wear. Have you noticed my robe?

*Angel:* Well, yes, as a matter of fact, it is quite lovely, and I wondered how you ever got such a robe.

*Mary:* Well, the robe is the righteousness of Jesus Christ and it was a free gift. He just gave it to me. I would never dare try to come into this throne room in my own clothes—they are truly filthy rags. Yet I wrap myself up in this gorgeous robe of the righteousness of Jesus, and because Jesus is acceptable to God, so am I. You see, God doesn't see my filthy rags; He sees only this lovely robe of righteousness. He has clothed me with the garments of salvation; He has covered me with the robe of righteousness (see Is 61:10). I'm so thankful for this robe. Otherwise, I could never enter His presence. Now, if you'll excuse me, I'd like to go on up to the throne.

*Angel:* Just one minute. Look at your feet; they're quite dirty. Are you going with dirty feet?

*Mary:* Well, I realize they look terrible, but you see, that's the part of me that gets dirty when I walk around this world out here. Yet Jesus said that once I had been cleansed all over, I didn't need to be cleansed again, except just to have my feet washed (see Jn 13:10). So, one of the first things I do when I get to the throne is ask God to wash my feet. He always does, so I leave here with really clean feet. Wait and see!

*Angel:* Do you think He'll recognize you when you get there? Surely He can't remember your name—you're just one of millions and millions.

*Mary:* I know, but because He is God, He does know who I am. He always recognizes me right away. He even knows the number of hairs on my head (see Mt 10:30). He counts the times I sit and stand each day (see Ps 139:2). He puts my tears in a jar (see Ps 56:8). He wrote all my days in a book even before I was born (see Ps 139:16), and He is intimately acquainted with all my ways (see Ps 139:3).

*Angel:* Why would He want to know the number of hairs on your head—or care about everything you do?

*Mary:* Now that question I really can't answer. I've asked Him that many times myself, and He just smiles and says He calls all the stars by name (see Ps 147:4) and sees every sparrow that falls (see Mt 10:29), so surely He cares for me. Excuse me, I think He's waiting for me.

As I begin to walk down the glorious path that takes me up to the throne, the whole room gets quiet. The angels look at one another and ask, "Who is she? How did she get in here?" Yet no one can stop me, and I walk right up to that throne—yes, even with boldness.

As I get there I look up and say, "God, it's me, Mary." He looks down and recognizes me instantly. I thank Him for making it possible for me to come right to the throne and have fellowship with Him. He reminds me again that He delights in my fellowship; He created me for His pleasure. He rejoices over me with singing, and I am welcomed to take my place beside Him in that glorious throne, where I find mercy and grace to help me in my time of need (see Heb 4:16).

## See Yourself in Christ

So, if your self-image is suffering, if the world around you is trying to diminish your value, if your past is parading its ugly scenes in your head to remind you of your failures, if you are condemning yourself and allowing others to do so as well, please change your glasses! Please pick up those Forever Eyes and see the truth about who you are in Christ. Tuck these verses away in the memory banks of your mind, and remember they are the truth that will set you free and allow you to see yourself as God sees you, with Forever Eyes:

> *I have been crucified with Christ and I no longer live, but Christ lives in me. The life I live in the body, I live by faith in the Son of God, who loved me and gave himself for me.*
>
> GALATIANS 2:20

*For you died, and your life is now hidden with Christ in God.*

COLOSSIANS 3:3

*But because of his great love for us, God, who is rich in mercy, made us alive with Christ even when we were dead in transgressions—it is by grace you have been saved. And God raised us up with Christ and seated us with him in the heavenly realms in Christ Jesus, in order that in the coming ages he might show the incomparable riches of his grace, expressed in his kindness to us in Christ Jesus.*

EPHESIANS 2:4-7

**Three**

# Looking at People
# With *Forever* Eyes

As I think back over the almost twenty years I've been broadcasting on Christian radio and the more than twenty years I've been involved in women's ministries at my church, there's no doubt that the majority of struggles brought to my attention are people-related. This is true whether they are workplace issues, home issues, church issues, or world issues! The people in our lives become the source of our greatest struggles.

Just imagine, if you can, that you could change every person in your life so that each one was just the way you wanted him or her to be. By a stroke of your wand, you could make irritating habits go away; you could change attitudes; you could improve work habits; you could instill wisdom and goodness in people. Does it not cause your heart to miss a beat to even imagine such a scenario? How much happier your life would be! How much easier your life would be! Just imagine!

Don't spend much time there, however, because this is a dream world. We all know that we can't change people. I'm learning how terribly difficult it is to change myself, and I have the power to do that! Changing others truly is beyond me.

My last book, *Getting Along With People at Work*, is a treatise on how to deal with people. In that book I go into much detail on what we can and should do to improve relationships. Certainly the Bible gives us a great deal of guidance in this area, and I have tried to flesh it out

43

in such a way that we can put biblical principles into practice in dealing with people.

Here, however, my purpose is different, as we deal with people. It is to cause us to see the people in our lives through a totally different perspective than we normally do.

### Looking at Difficult People With Forever Eyes

Recently a good friend was telling me about her struggle with her boss. She is a good and valuable worker, and any boss in his or her right mind would be delighted to have her on the team. However, this particular boss treats her with great disrespect and causes much unnecessary stress and pressure on the job, not only for her but also for everyone who deals with him.

She said to me, "I'm not used to this kind of behavior. I was raised in a good home where we treated people with respect. I have a good marriage with a husband who is kind and who never raises his voice to me. I just don't know how to deal with people like my boss."

I said to her, "You know, I have a similar background. My parents were good and loving. I was raised in a wholesome atmosphere with good values and much respect. Yet what I'm learning is that my experience is most likely the exception and not the rule these days. Therefore, I see the world through different eyes than most people do because of my very well-balanced beginning."

Then I asked her, "Do you think that God may have led you to this very job, working for this very man, because He wants you to see how the other half of the world lives? Could it be that God's purpose for allowing you to endure this unfair and unkind treatment is to educate you about what most of the people you deal with have had to come through? Maybe God wants you to be aware of just how blessed you have been and to appreciate His goodness to you even more."

In order to do that, my friend will have to look at this man with Forever Eyes, and knowing her, she will set her will to do that. Yet it will have to be an intentional decision on her part, because she is the one who has to deal with him on a day-to-day basis, and she will be sorely tempted to see him through her own earthly eyes. It won't be easy, but it will be greatly beneficial.

It's easy to see the good people in our lives with Forever Eyes. As I have indicated, my parents were the kind of parents every child should have. My brothers are the best brothers any sister could have. My daughter and son-in-law are a great joy to me. My extended family of nieces and nephews are nothing but a blessing to our family. I can look at all of these people and immediately see God's wonderful hand of goodness in allowing me to be a part of this family. That's easy to do.

Yet what about the difficult people? Or the good ones who are difficult at times or in certain areas? That's where my ability to look with Forever Eyes is sorely tested. I can easily see how a person affects my life in negative ways. It's not so easy to see that same person in a different light.

For example, imagine this hypothetical situation: You work in an office with five other people, and the job is busy and demanding. Everyone gets along pretty well, except for Joan, whose desk is right next to yours. (My apologies to all Joans for randomly choosing your name in this example.) Joan is not so easy to get along with. She talks all the time, and doesn't have a whole lot to say, if you know what I mean. She's loud, she grumbles and complains a lot, and she spends time doing personal things and goofing off, so you have to carry some of her workload. Joan is no picnic.

In order to tolerate Joan, you've started ignoring her. You go home at night and grumble about all the irritating things she's done each day, feeling sorry for yourself, feeling misused, and you've finally come to the place where you just don't speak to her unless you absolutely have to. Of course, everyone else also treats Joan that way, or worse, so you know it's not just your problem.

Now suppose that the next time you go to work, you decide to intentionally look at Joan through Forever Eyes. What would you see? You would see invisible things, like her soul. That soul is going to live forever; it is eternal. And you might also see a broken heart. With Joan's aggressive behavior, you probably never realized that underneath is a broken heart. It takes Forever Eyes to see broken hearts. Do you wonder why Joan's heart is so broken and painful? Have you ever tried to find out? Have you ever taken her to lunch and just let her talk to you?

When you wear Forever Eyes, people look different, because you see them the way God sees them. You know, God loves Joan just as much as He loves you. Oh, He doesn't necessarily love her behavior, but then God's love is not based on our behavior. Aren't you glad? Where would you and I be, if it were?

If you started looking at Joan through Forever Eyes, how would it change your behavior? You'd be more patient; you'd be able to say nice things to her and be civil to her. You would no longer cringe when she walked into the room, because you'd see beyond her behavior. Imagine the stress that would be removed from your own life. I wonder if your changed behavior toward Joan might even cause her to make some needed changes. It could happen.

In a job I had many years ago, I had to learn to look at my boss through Forever Eyes. It took me the better part of a year to relinquish my self-pity and my right for revenge and tell the Lord that I wanted to see this man the way He saw him. During that year I rebelled against having to work for this boss; I complained and griped about him to all of my friends; I went to work every day expecting to be miserable because of him, and I was.

Finally realizing that God wasn't going to let me out of that job until I had learned some valuable lessons, I began to pray for Forever Eyes. God loves to answer that prayer. I remember so well how different it was to go into a meeting with this man after I looked at him with Forever Eyes. As I sat there listening to his words and directions that had so angered and embittered me before, I began to feel sorry for him. I could see his insecurities; I could see his desperate need for recognition; I could see his unfulfilled and discontented life. I recognized that he didn't have the power of God's Spirit in his life, because he was not rightly related to Jesus Christ, and I truly felt sorry for him.

### Looking at Different People With Forever Eyes

Not long ago I received an e-mail from a listener to my radio broadcast who was having difficulty with one of her coworkers. Her job involved daily travel by car with her coworkers, up to three or four hours each day. She had discovered that one of the men newly hired was homosexual, and the thought of having to spend hours with him gave her "the creeps," to use her words. She was contemplating quitting her job rather than having to be in such close quarters with this man. She asked me for advice on how to handle this relationship. Here is part of my reply to her:

A homosexual man is a man loved by God who desperately needs to know God and find freedom from his sexual sin.... I would encourage you to ask God to help you see him the way

God sees him. God loves him as much as He loves you, and he doesn't give God "the creeps."

There are many people with whom you work who are sinners—living in known sin. It's just that this particular sin is difficult for you to accept or understand. But it is no greater sin to God than any other.

I don't believe people are in our lives by accident. And one of the challenges we face as Christians in the workplace is to share God's love with whomever God brings along our way.

Do you not think that if you can begin to see this man as God sees him, you might have an opportunity to show him that we Christians are not gay-bashers or haters—as they think we are—and that we can truly love them and know them as people, not as homosexuals? I'm not suggesting we compromise our stand toward the sin of homosexuality, but keep remembering that his problem is that he needs to know Jesus.

I don't know what God wants you to do, but I would urge you to really seek God's view on this. This could be a life-changing relationship for you and him. But you will have to see him as God sees him.... God may have placed you in this situation "for such a time as this." Don't let your fears and emotions keep you from looking through Forever Eyes. You could miss a great blessing.

Not long afterward she e-mailed me again and affirmed that she was indeed taking my challenge to see this man through Forever Eyes. Her attitude toward him had already changed, just by making that one decision, and I could sense that God had started a new work in her heart.

## Looking at Relationship Problems With Forever Eyes

In Philippians 4 the apostle Paul writes:

> *I plead with Euodia and I plead with Syntyche to agree with each other in the Lord. Yes, and I ask you, loyal yokefellow, help these women who have contended at my side in the cause of the gospel, along with Clement and the rest of my fellow workers, whose names are in the book of life.*
>
> PHILIPPIANS 4:2-3

How would you like to have a personal spat recorded in Scripture for all time? I wonder how many millions of people have read about Euodia and Syntyche's falling out. Evidently it was serious enough for Paul to address it openly, but it had to be embarrassing for these two women when that letter was read out loud to the church at Philippi.

Now, imagine if you will that you meet Euodia in heaven, and you ask her, "What was the problem you and Syntyche had?" My guess is she'll look at you with a blank stare. "What problem?" she'll ask. "You know, the one Paul wrote about in the fourth chapter of Philippians." Do you think either of them will remember what caused this disagreement? I doubt it.

Is there someone in your life right now with whom you are having a "spat"? It might be an outward, verbal one, or it could be a quiet one, where you simply have distanced yourself from each other. You know there's a problem when the presence of the other person makes you uncomfortable; when you go out of your way to avoid that person; when you find yourself gossiping about him or her; when you've thrown a pity party or two over that person. Anybody come to mind?

Now, transport yourself from this life and see yourself in eternity, in heaven. Will that person be there too? Does he or she know Jesus personally? If not, how important is that spat, or your hurt feelings, or your rights being trampled upon, compared to his or her eternal destiny?

Back to the Euodia and Syntyche squabble: These are two sisters in Christ. How can two family members be at each other's throats? Well, we all know full well how that can happen, both in our heavenly family and in our earthly family. I have known several people who desperately wanted to find a job in a Christian organization or a church because they were under the false impression that Christians never had relationship struggles. Of course, they were quickly disillusioned when they discovered that even fellow Christians can have irritating habits, sharp tongues, poor work habits, and disagreeable personalities.

Whatever the cause of these relationship difficulties, do you really think it will be of any consequence in heaven? I don't mean that we are to totally ignore the causes of trouble here on earth. I know some things have to be confronted and discussed. Yet before we get to that stage, if we can learn to look at our relationship troubles through Forever Eyes and recognize their lack of significance in light of eternity, it will not only change our attitude but also greatly enhance the probability of reconciliation. When you approach a difficult relationship with Forever Eyes, your words, your body language, and your objectives are immensely different—changed for the better.

### Looking at Unbelievers With Forever Eyes

It can be easy for us to develop wrong attitudes toward people who are not yet believers. We may have a pompous, self-righteous attitude toward them. We may see their sinful lifestyles and become judgmental and critical. Or they may seem to be getting away with their sin and enjoying a success and freedom from trouble that we don't have, even though we are trying to live out our faith in integrity and truth. We may become envious rather quickly if we look through only earthly eyes.

Proverbs 24:19 says: "Do not fret because of evil men or be envious of the wicked, for the evil man has no future hope, and the lamp of the wicked will be snuffed out." Stop and look beyond the present to the end of the story. That person who is not yet a believer has no future hope! Grab that thought and meditate on it for a few minutes—no future hope! Where would you be without a future hope? What do you think you would be like without the assurance that your eternal destiny is secure because of Jesus?

I often remind myself of what a miserable person I would be on my own. I would be totally self-consumed; I would be constantly fighting for my rights; I would be power hungry and overly ambitious; I would be uncaring about others, especially those who didn't suit me—just to mention a few. I've seen enough of myself to get a glimpse of what I would be like without Jesus. Take my word for it—you wouldn't like me!

In Psalm 73, Asaph had to change his entire perspective as he looked at the "prosperity of the wicked." Looking with his earthly eyes, he thought that these wicked people had no struggles, were healthy and strong, and were free from burdens and illness. Even though they were arrogant and callous in their attitude toward God, they still seemed to prosper, without punishment.

"Surely in vain have I kept my heart pure; in vain have I washed my hands in innocence," Asaph moans (v. 13). Through his earthly eyes, Asaph saw those unbelievers and became angry, envious, and disgusted. "My feet had almost slipped; I had nearly lost my foothold," he declares (v. 2). That's what earthly eyes will do to you, especially when you see that evil people are more prosperous and successful than you are.

However, Asaph was able to keep from slipping by entering the sanctuary of God: "Then I understood their final destiny," he says (v. 17). He looked into eternity and saw their end. Without God the unbelievers were doomed to ruin; they would be destroyed—and that for eternity. Asaph looked with Forever Eyes, and it totally changed his view of those people without God. "But as for me, it is good to be near God. I have made the Sovereign Lord my refuge; I will tell of all your deeds," he affirms as he closes that psalm (v. 28).

No doubt some of you have unbelievers—or even evil people—in your life who create some temporary havoc for you. A boss, a mate, a child, a parent, a friend—they come in all forms. When we encounter these people, our natural, human tendency is to focus on the problems they are creating for us at the moment.

That is when we must intentionally enter into God's presence. Thankfully, His sanctuary is no longer limited to a certain location; we can enter His presence with boldness, any time, anywhere, because Jesus has opened the curtain into the Holy of Holies. We call this process of entering God's presence prayer, and it is our greatest privilege as children of God.

The hard part is being willing to give up the pity party, the anger, the self-focus, and go into God's presence. Once we do that, however, and begin to pray for Forever Eyes, we will see these people's final destiny. The Bible says there is no other way to God except through Jesus Christ, and therefore without Christ there is no hope for eternity. That means an eternity of separation from God, an eternity of unquenchable thirst, an eternity of unfulfilled and ever-increasing desires and passions. Have you thought about eternity in hell lately? Put on your Forever Eyes and look at it. It will cause you to tremble. That is what awaits anyone not rightly related to God through Jesus Christ.

Forever Eyes give you a completely changed view of the irritating, difficult nonbeliever. Because "God has poured out his love into our hearts by the Holy Spirit" (Rom 5:5), Forever Eyes will give us compassion and empathy, and yes, even love for the unbelievers in our lives.

## Looking Through Eyes of Love

As I write this book, my focus for this year comes from 1 Corinthians 13:8, "Love never fails," and from 1 Corinthians 16:14, "Do everything in love." Putting these together, Paul tells us to operate out of love all the time, because love will never fail. So, I'm focusing on putting that into practice in my everyday life. Less than three months into this year, I can tell you of multiple failures already. Yet I will not give up. I want to learn to do everything out of a heart of love. When we relate to others out of love, our efforts will never fail. They will never fail to heal, to calm, to transform relationships. Love never fails. Name any other relationship tactic that is guaranteed never to fail.

I've written extensively about confrontations, because they are a necessary part of life. Yet each time I warn that confrontation may not help. There's no guarantee, even if you confront constructively, that the other person will receive it. Confrontations sometimes fail.

Negotiation is another good skill to use in dealing with people. Good businesspeople, as well as many moms, are very good at negotiating differences, finding some middle ground, and pacifying both parties in a dispute. Yet negotiations can fail. There's no guarantee of success.

Even sympathy and empathy can fail. I've taught lots of people in my business training seminars how to deal with angry people, and you always begin with empathy or sympathy. It almost always helps to calm the angry person down. Yet it doesn't work all the time.

However, operating out of a heart of genuine love never fails. The challenge is this: How in the world do you do that in the heat of the moment, when your emotions are going in the opposite direction? You train yourself to look with Forever Eyes and see the end.

I tell you, it's the most amazing transformation. When I practice it, I'm in awe at what happens to me. God changes me! It's great to hear about how God has changed other people, but how much more marvelous it is to recognize significant changes in yourself. Loving people you don't like would be mission impossible without Forever Eyes.

Looking with Forever Eyes causes instant maturation! It grows you up real fast, and gives you the power to overlook any temporary unpleasantness. Proverbs 12:16 says, "A fool shows his annoyance at once, but a prudent man overlooks an insult." If you study the definition of a fool, as given by wise Solomon in the book of Proverbs, you'll quickly figure out that foolish people never have an eternal perspective. They are totally focused on what's happening to them at the moment, how it makes them feel, what they want now, and how they can get it. They have no long-term view, and this is their destruction.

A prudent person is one who is wisely cautious. The dictionary defines prudent as "careful in providing for the future," and a synonym for prudence is foresight or forethought. A prudent person can overlook an insult, because a prudent person is looking with Forever Eyes. You can't overlook an insult or a hurt someone has tried to inflict on you if you see with only earthly eyes. Yet as soon as you put on Forever Eyes, you can look beyond an insult, not reacting to it, not lowering yourself to the other person's level, not acting like an immature child.

Another great benefit in learning to see people with Forever Eyes is that you will see potential and possibilities you would never otherwise see. With our earthly eyes we often discount people based on their looks. There are certain stereotypes that have been emblazoned in our minds through our culture that cause us to see people in prejudiced ways.

For example, someone who is significantly overweight is usually viewed as less intelligent, less sophisticated, less successful or capable. Someone who is very short, particularly a man, is seen as less important, less mature. A person who dresses inappropriately, who has an untidy appearance, causes us to form a negative impression about him or her.

We can talk until we're blue in the face about not judging books by their covers, but as long as we look at people with only earthly eyes, we will never completely avoid this tendency. It is as old as time.

The story of how Samuel anointed David as the coming king illustrates the point. You'll find it recorded in 1 Samuel 16. God told Samuel that He had selected one of Jesse's sons to be king over Israel, and Samuel was to go and select the chosen one. He arrived in Bethlehem and invited Jesse and his sons to join him as he sacrificed to the Lord.

The first son he saw was Eliab, and immediately he thought Eliab was the chosen one because he was the firstborn, and he was good-looking and tall. "Surely the Lord's anointed stands here before the Lord," Samuel said (v. 6). "But the Lord said to Samuel, 'Do not consider his appearance or his height, for I have rejected him. The Lord does not look at the things man looks at. Man looks at the outward appearance, but the Lord looks at the heart'" (v. 7).

One by one Samuel examined Jesse's sons, seven of them, but after he had looked each of them over he said, "The Lord has not chosen these" (v. 10). He asked Jesse if these were all his sons.

"There is still the youngest," Jesse answered, "but he is tending the sheep." Samuel said, "Send for him; we will not sit down until he arrives" (v. 11).

It was obvious that Jesse never thought David would be selected.

He had not even brought him in from the fields. He had seven older sons, good-looking, accomplished, qualified. Why would Samuel pass over the seven sons and ask for the youngest—the shepherd boy?

As soon as David arrived, the Lord instructed Samuel to anoint him as the coming king, with the other brothers looking on. I can imagine the jealousy that each of those seven boys must have felt at that time. David was the youngest; David was doing the lowliest of work, tending sheep. David was not as educated or experienced or mature as the other seven. Why David?

Because God looks at people differently than we do. He sees beyond the outward appearance and looks at the heart. As Samuel was informed, "The Lord does not look at the things man looks at" (v. 7).

Through many years of business training, countless times I have taught the commonly accepted belief that perception equals reality. What people see or think becomes their reality, whether it is factually true or not. Therefore, we must be concerned with appearances and first impressions because our success in the business world is in part dependent upon how people see us. I know from experience that this is true, and there is value in understanding that perception equals reality.

However, looking at people with Forever Eyes changes that common saying considerably. In fact, what the Lord said to Samuel, in today's vernacular, was: Perception does *not* equal reality. What you see is not what you get. If we are ever going to see people the way God does, we will have to become very intentional about shedding this "perception equals reality" idea, at least in the way we look at others.

I'm convinced that in heaven we will be shocked to see who is on the front row, so to speak. It will for the most part be people we've never heard of, people who received little or no recognition here on earth, people who would not have passed our qualification test or our critical analysis. Yet in God's eyes they are winners because of their heart condition.

I could name several people I personally know whom I've come to see with Forever Eyes. If I introduced them to you, you would not be impressed with their appearance. If you talked with them, they would not amaze you with their intellects. If you read their resumes, you might be bored. Yet if you could see them with Forever Eyes, you would see servant attitudes. You would see joyful spirits. You would see faithful service. You would see loving hearts.

I think of one woman whose personal appearance is not impressive, indeed just the opposite. I can remember a time when I was almost embarrassed to introduce her at our church functions. Sad to say, I remember thinking, "She is not a good representation of the women in our church. She doesn't make a good impression." (That says more about me than it does about her.)

Yet I see her now with Forever Eyes, and I love to see her coming. She is a delight and she is always giving to and thinking of others. Her spirit is positive, and her faithfulness is legendary. I'd love for you to meet her.

We miss many wonderful relationships and we overlook some very gifted and effective people when we don't see them with Forever Eyes. We allow our earthly eyes to control our opinions and impressions of others. This is not only a fault on our part, it is also foolish, because we miss some "Davids," some people after God's own heart.

I hope you are beginning to get an inkling of how powerful Forever Eyes are. Since relationships are the sandpaper of our lives, and most of our issues in life are related to people, looking at people with Forever Eyes is one of our best stress reducers, and it can improve our people skills immensely.

**Four**

# Looking at Desires
# With *Forever* Eyes

Esau never seemed to look with Forever Eyes. He was consumed with the here and now, with having what he wanted when he wanted it. With his twin brother, Jacob, he grew up and became a skillful hunter and a man of the outdoors. Here is the familiar story of his downfall:

> *Once when Jacob was cooking some stew, Esau came in from the open country, famished. He said to Jacob, "Quick, let me have some of that red stew! I'm famished!" (That is why he was also called Edom.)*
>
> *Jacob replied, "First sell me your birthright."*
>
> *"Look, I am about to die," Esau said. "What good is the birthright to me?"*
>
> *But Jacob said, "Swear to me first." So he swore an oath to him, selling his birthright to Jacob.*
>
> *Then Jacob gave Esau some bread and some lentil stew. He ate and drank, and then got up and left.*
>
> *So Esau despised his birthright.*
>
> GENESIS 25:29-34

Esau sold the eternal for the temporary. That birthright was his because he was the firstborn, and it guaranteed to him the legacy of his father, Isaac. He was in line to receive his father's special blessing and the major inheritance of his earthly goods, as well as the position of spiritual head of the family. In our culture it is difficult for us to appreciate the value of this birthright, for there is nothing that compares to it exactly. Yet it would be similar to forfeiting a great fortune and a place of prominence for yourself and your children.

Esau knew the importance of that birthright, but in a moment of hunger he could see only his temporary need. I have wondered if Jacob's stew was the only food in the place. Surely in an affluent home such as theirs was, Esau could have found something else to eat. He could have cooked his own stew. Sure, it would have taken a little time, but Esau was not truly at starvation's door.

People have fasted for many days without dying. Our Lord fasted forty days and nights. Missing a few meals is not a death sentence. Yet, Esau seemed to believe that if he didn't get a meal at that moment, he would die. What utter nonsense!

Esau wanted what he wanted when he wanted it. And he was willing to relinquish the valuable, incredibly important birthright for a bowl of stew. He gave up that which counted for eternity for that which lasted only a moment.

How soon would he be hungry again? In a few hours, no doubt. So, what he received in exchange for his eternal birthright had no lasting value.

How was Esau so deceived that he was willing to do this? What could cause a man to be so terribly shortsighted? Well, you see, Esau told himself a lie and he believed it. "I am about to die," he said. The hunger pangs sent him a message that he chose to interpret incorrectly. That's how he deceived himself so that he could justify his decision to fork over the birthright for a bowl of stew.

No doubt Esau thought he was making a free choice as he opted for the stew, but in reality, he was a slave to his appetite. That appetite blotted out eternity for him, and he paid a very large price for it.

It's true that Jacob doesn't come off as a knight in shining armor in this story, for he took full advantage of Esau's weakness. But Jacob knew the eternal value of that birthright, and he saw his opportunity to gain it for himself. Though his tactics are not admirable, his vision is.

Keep in mind, Esau could never have been swindled if he had said "no" to Jacob's deal. It was Esau's lack of vision and his absorption with his present need, his desire for instant gratification, that cost him his most treasured possession.

## When Needs Become Addictions

Esau is a good lesson for us in the importance of looking with Forever Eyes. How often are we guilty of poor choices because we look at only the here and now. We settle for temporary satisfaction at the cost of eternal pleasures. Let's face it—we all have Esau natures, wanting what we want when we want it! And we're all pretty good at deceiving ourselves when we want to. We tell ourselves lies about our needs, and believe our own lies, of course.

As a single woman, I well remember the gnawing need I had to find a man. As I gave in to that need, I made many poor choices over a ten-year period, because the here-and-now need occupied my mind. The more I thought about my singleness and its disadvantages, the more I became a slave to that need. It led to an addiction, much like Esau's addiction to his appetite. And like Esau, I lied to myself and believed my lies.

I thought life could not be meaningful or satisfactory as a single woman. I had many other single women to support my theory, for they believed the same lie, and so I made poor choice after poor choice, trying to meet my immediate need without ever looking with Forever Eyes.

Like Esau, my need was a normal one. Esau was hungry for food; I was hungry for love and relationship. These are legitimate needs that must be acknowledged. Yet when we look at our legitimate needs through only earthly eyes, we will often become addicted to them. And then what God intended for good in our lives becomes a stumbling block and an entry point for sinful choices.

Certainly the enemy of our souls uses this propensity very effectively, because, unwittingly, we aid and abet him. If we continue to look at our needs through earthly eyes, it is a shortcut from there for Satan to turn that need into an addiction. Before we know it, we are convinced that we cannot make it without meeting that need here and now, in any way possible.

When I made the decision to turn the control of my life back over to the Lord Jesus Christ, I had to be delivered from my addiction, and it didn't happen overnight. Yet I was absolutely serious about the commitment, so the Lord and I worked through it. Though at the time I didn't think of my need for love and relationship as an addiction, in retrospect I believe it was indeed that. An addiction that I brought on myself by allowing a legitimate need to become the most important desire in my life.

Because I journaled my way through this time period, I can retrace my steps. I well remember the day—and it took about eighteen months to get to that point—when I was walking down the streets of Chicago feeling free and joyful. Suddenly I thought, "You're happy; how did that happen?" for I had thought I could never be really happy being single! I realized then that I was free from this addiction. I could honestly say that it didn't matter whether I was single or married. My life was in the hands of the eternal God, and I could trust Him to work the best for me.

This healing from my addiction came as I determined to see my life and its future through Forever Eyes. Twenty years later, as I now try to recall that addictive period of my life, I can hardly believe that I willingly subjected myself to such torment for ten long years. I now enjoy freedom, contentment, and a fulfilling life, but it could have been mine much sooner if I had looked at my own life situation with Forever Eyes.

Now, as I often talk to and counsel women in similar situations, I try to find the words that will persuade them to look with Forever Eyes and recognize that their need does not have to make them into victims. Yet I must report that I don't have a great track record in turning others around. This blindness we have when we are addicted to a need in our lives is extremely powerful.

I remember talking with one young single woman about her overwhelming desire to be married. She could not imagine ever being free from that need; she could not believe that life could ever be meaningful for her unless she married. I urged her to just give God permission to change that desire if that was His will, even though she didn't honestly believe that even God could do that.

## Finding Deliverance From Addictions

When we are in the grips of a normal need that has become an addiction, we often cannot believe that there is any escape other than having that need met. How do you make yourself believe that you can be delivered from an addiction? You can't. Yet you must take your faith as far as you can at that point in time. Pray that if God can deliver you,

you give Him permission to do so. Pray that God will make you want to be delivered. Start right where you are.

I often think of the man who came to Jesus with his demon-possessed son, hoping he could be healed. He said to Jesus:

> *"But if you can do anything, take pity on us and help us."*
>
> *"If you can?" said Jesus. "Everything is possible for him who believes."*
>
> *Immediately the boy's father exclaimed, "I do believe; help me overcome my unbelief!"*

MARK 9:22b-24

The man wasn't sure that Jesus could heal his son, but he was desperate enough to ask. And then he even had the nerve to ask Jesus to help him overcome his unbelief so that his faith would be enough for his son's healing. An audacious request, wouldn't you agree? Yet Jesus honored it.

Many times in my own life I've had to ask Jesus to help me overcome my unbelief. Many times I've prayed for the faith that I need to do what God wants me to do. It is just another indication that in myself I have no power to meet my needs or solve my problems. I can't even work up the faith I need to trust God.

You'd think that our heavenly Father would be disgusted by this type of request. You'd think He would say, "When you can get your act together and truly have faith in me, then come make your requests. But until then, I don't want to hear from you." Yet our God is not like that.

Psalm 103 reminds us that, "As a father has compassion on his children, so the Lord has compassion on those who fear him; for he knows how we are formed, he remembers that we are dust" (Ps 103:13-14). God doesn't expect a whole lot from us in our natural human condition. So, when we readily admit our inability to have the faith we need, it doesn't shock Him. He is such a compassionate Father that He willingly answers our request for more faith, if we just ask.

At one point the apostles said to the Lord, "Increase our faith!" He replied, "If you have faith as small as a mustard seed, you can say to this mulberry tree, 'Be uprooted and planted in the sea,' and it will obey you" (Lk 17:5-6). The Lord Jesus repeatedly taught His disciples that even with minute amounts of faith they could see wondrous displays of His power.

Asking for the faith we need to believe God is often where we have to begin, and our God is faithful to take us up right at that weak point and implant faith in our hearts. It may be a very small amount, but He can work with it if we are sincere in our desire to have faith in Him and to be delivered from our addictions.

## Eternity in Your Heart

In a wonderful little devotional book called *A Diary of Private Prayer*, John Ballie writes: "I thank Thee, O Lord, that Thou has so set eternity within my heart that no earthly thing can ever satisfy me wholly."[1] As Augustine said, "Thou has made us for Thyself, and our hearts are restless until they find their rest in Thee."

There's an old song that Peggy Lee made famous called "Is That All There Is?" She sings about having a number of incredible experiences, some good, some bad. At the end of each experience, she feels a great disappointment and sings, "Is that all there is? Is that all there is? If that's all there is, my friend, then let's keep dancing, if that's all there is." The song personifies the disillusionment of life.

Many people are singing their own versions of that song. They spend their lives, their resources, their energy pursuing what they think will meet their needs, only to discover when they reach those goals that the victory is empty. Is that all there is? The desires and needs that drove them to abandon the future for the present fail to live up to their promise. The high price they have paid for that here-and-now gratification and satisfaction proves to be a poor investment. Like Esau, once the stomach is full, the realization of what they have given up for temporary satisfaction covers them like a dark cloud.

The wise Solomon wrote:

> *He has made everything beautiful in its time. He has also set eternity in the hearts of men; yet they cannot fathom what God has done from beginning to end.*
>
> ECCLESIASTES 3:11

Eternity has been set in your heart. You are born with the instinctual knowledge that there is more than this present life, and that eternity is far more important than the here and now. Even people who never think about God, who don't even believe in God, have eternity in their hearts. They may deny it or ignore it, but it is there!

Paul wrote to the Romans:

> *For since the creation of the world God's invisible qualities—his eternal power and divine nature—have been clearly seen, being understood from what has been made, so that men are without excuse.*
>
> ROMANS 1:20

What do you think drives people to addictions of all kinds, to poor choices, to wrong behavior? They are seeking satisfaction in the inner person. They are looking for something to quench that insatiable thirst, something to stop the pain, something to ease the longing. Their desires have driven them to look wherever they think they might find satisfaction. Yet, as Ballie writes, no earthly thing can ever satisfy us wholly because eternity is in our hearts.

## View Your Needs Through Forever Eyes

Our continual challenge is to see our legitimate needs and desires from God's perspective. When we do, we can endure unmet needs without selling our birthrights. We can look forward to the day when God will supply all of our needs and meet our deepest heart's desires. We can learn to find our desires and needs met in ways we never thought possible, healthy and holy ways.

No wonder David was a man after God's own heart, for in spite of his many failings, he understood this truth. He writes:

*You have made known to me the path of life;*
*you will fill me with joy in your presence,*
*with eternal pleasures at your right hand.*

PSALM 16:11

Eternal pleasures are found at the right hand of God. When we're willing to settle for mere earthly pleasures, we're in the Esau camp. Eternal pleasures can be seen only with Forever Eyes, but they are real and they are lasting.

Earthly pleasures often leave us more than just empty; they leave us filled with regret and guilt. The enticement of our flesh and our lust looks very promising to our earthly eyes, but the aftermath can leave us with a suitcase full of baggage to carry with us for weeks and months—even years—to come.

Moses also learned to wear Forever Eyes:

*By faith Moses, when he had grown up, refused to be known as the son of Pharaoh's daughter. He chose to be mistreated along with the people of God rather than to enjoy the pleasures of sin for a short time. He regarded disgrace for the sake of Christ as of greater value than the treasures of Egypt, because he was looking ahead to his reward.*

HEBREWS 11:24-26

He was looking ahead—that is why Moses chose to follow the Lord God rather than go after the gods of Egypt. The pleasures of sin are there, but they last a short time and leave a terrible taste in your mouth. Eternal pleasures come without baggage—no regrets, no guilt.

In another psalm, David writes:

*Praise the Lord, O my soul,*
*and forget not all his benefits—*
*who forgives all your sins*
*and heals all your diseases,*
*who redeems your life from the pit*
*and crowns you with love and compassion,*
*who satisfies your desires with good things*
*so that your youth is renewed like the eagle's.*

PSALM 103:2-5

When we look for the eternal pleasures found in God's presence, our desires are satisfied with good things. When we look to the lures and attractions of this world and are deceived by their enticements, we are trying to satisfy our desires with bad things, and it simply never works, at least not for long.

## The Freedom of Forever Eyes

What freedom Forever Eyes give us! How can I describe it adequately so that, if you've not yet relinquished your desires to God, you will be motivated to do so now? Remember that your needs are sending you false messages, just as Esau's appetite did. You can have a good and meaningful life without illicit sex, without a marriage partner if God so wills, without a fat bank account, without a power position, without fame or recognition.

Can you even imagine how much easier your life would be if you were not addicted to some need or desire? Just think of being free from that driving emotion, not spending every waking minute thinking about it, not being tempted to do what you know is wrong. Wouldn't you like to wake up in the mornings without that addictive need jamming your thought life and controlling your actions?

That's what the apostle Paul is talking about in Romans 6 when he reminds us that we are slaves either to sin or to righteousness. If we do not choose to be a "slave to righteousness," we will default our lives to be slaves to sin. There's no in-between here. "You have been set free from sin and have become slaves to righteousness," he writes in verse 18. "But now that you have been set free from sin and have become slaves to God, the benefit you reap leads to holiness, and the result is eternal life" (v. 22).

The benefit of choosing to be a slave to righteousness rather than defaulting to become a slave to sin is an eternal one. Being a slave to righteousness simply means choosing to do the right thing at every turning point in our lives. With Forever Eyes we can see clearly the eternal benefits that are ours when we refuse to allow our needs and desires to drive us into harmful and sinful choices.

This freedom is ours for the choosing. If you are not yet living in freedom from your addiction, it is because you're deceiving yourself into believing that you can't live without it. At any time in any day, you can choose to abandon that addiction, and with God's grace find the freedom that is rightfully yours in Christ Jesus. I challenge you to find one good reason why you would not want to do that.

**Five**

# Looking at Success
# With *Forever* Eyes

I was born with a very competitive spirit. Well, that's a nice way to put it. The truth is, I always want to win; I always want to be number one; I am a very bad loser.

I found that my competitive spirit came in handy in my career. As I entered the world of IBM sales, one of the first women in that position, my drive to win kept me going on many discouraging days. There was an eternal quota hanging over my head, and I was evaluated and paid according to my ability to reach and exceed that monthly quota. There was much recognition and reward for those who succeeded. I wanted to succeed.

IBM counted on having a sales force that was competitive and hated losing. The company established many incentives to keep us working hard, selling somebody something! In those days it was known as the premiere sales organization in American business, and I was proud to be a part of that team.

### Fighting the Performance Mentality

Looking at success with Forever Eyes is not easy for me. I have a performance mentality indelibly stamped in my brain that keeps saying that success is numbers and achievements and honors and recognition. It has to do with my performance!

From birth on we discover that much of our success and our value is based on our performance. We quickly learn that our performance determines whether we have or have not; whether we win or lose; whether we succeed or fail. Before babies can talk we're telling them they're good boys or good girls, or bad boys or bad girls, based on their behavior.

Once we start to school, we learn that our performance determines our grades. Our grades determine whether we are promoted or not. Our school record determines what college we can attend. We have to perform in order to achieve academic success.

Even with our parents and family, we can find that love is given or withheld based on performance. It should not be true, but it happens. I get many letters from people who are still today very injured because they couldn't perform to their parent's expectations and they lost their approval and sometimes their love because of poor performance. So, many people think they have to perform in order to earn love.

This happens with mates as well. People get married and then find that their mate has performance expectations. When they don't or can't live up to them, love, devotion, and loyalty are withheld, and the marriage often breaks up because it was based on performance.

In most business settings we sit down annually with our managers and have our job performance critiqued. We are judged in these evaluations by certain standards that are set by our company or manager, and we are judged by comparison to others in similar jobs. Usually merit raises are dependent on how well we score in these performance evaluations, and promotions are earned by outstanding performance.

To live in a performance-driven world is to live in a state of legalism. Certain standards or expectations—or laws—are placed upon us, and we strive to abide and achieve. When we do, we feel good about ourselves. When we excel, we are very proud of ourselves. When we don't, we get down on ourselves and feel guilty.

Living in a performance-driven world leads us to lots of comparisons. If my performance is better than yours is, I feel I am better than you are. If I am better than lots of other people at something, I really feel good about myself and think I'm something special. If, on the other hand, you outperform me, I'm in trouble, because I base my worth on how I perform, compared to you or to someone else.

So, we judge success by performance and achievement, position and power, riches and possessions. God doesn't. Looking at success with Forever Eyes is a shocking revelation to our performance-driven minds.

### Success in Eternity

How will success be judged in eternity? That's what we want to focus on here. So, let's put on those Forever Eyes and take a look.

One of the greatest truths in Scripture is that salvation is by grace alone through faith, not by works. We secure a place in God's eternal heaven through faith in the finished work of Jesus Christ. Our entry into that place of bliss is determined by our relationship to the One who died to redeem us.

Yet few Christians stop to think about the fact that we will face a judgment in heaven. It's called the Judgment Seat of Christ, and it is a judgment for believers, not unbelievers. It will be conducted on the other side of eternity, after we have made the transition, and it is only for those who are spending eternity in heaven.

We will stand individually before Christ for our works to be judged. And at this Judgment Seat, what we have done that has no eternal significance or benefit will be burned up in fire. Here's what the apostle

Paul wrote to the Corinthians about the Judgment Seat:

*By the grace God has given me, I laid a foundation as an expert builder, and someone else is building on it. But each one should be careful how he builds. For no one can lay any foundation other than the one already laid, which is Jesus Christ. If any man builds on this foundation using gold, silver, costly stones, wood, hay or straw, his work will be shown for what it is, because the Day will bring it to light. It will be revealed with fire, and the fire will test the quality of each man's work. If what he has built survives, he will receive his reward. If it is burned up, he will suffer loss; he himself will be saved, but only as one escaping through the flames.*

1 CORINTHIANS 3:10-15

What we have done that has eternal significance will come through the fire, like gold and diamonds and precious stones that cannot be harmed by fire. Quality will be judged, not quantity.

Some will suffer loss at that Judgment Seat. Yes, they'll be in heaven; yes, they'll have eternity with God; yes, their sins will be forgiven and their pasts will be behind them. Yet they will suffer loss at the Judgment Seat, as everything goes up in smoke. It will be loss of rewards that will be given out. It will be loss of ruling and reigning in heaven.

These people will be saved, yet as one escaping through the flames—by the skin of their teeth, as we say. They'll be left with nothing to cast at the feet of Christ in worship, and they will suffer loss. I believe this is the place where tears will be wiped away, as many will be sorrowful at this Judgment Seat because they will finally see their lives from an eternal perspective, but it will be too late.

That's how success will be determined in eternity for all to see and know. We will be in for some shocking surprises as we see that many of the "big names" don't have as much that survives the fire and comes out as gold as do some humble, unknown people who lived their lives focused on eternal rather than earthly success.

The Judgment Seat of Christ is a sobering topic, and not one to give us warm fuzzies or cause joviality. Frankly, I'm tempted not to bring it up in this book because I want you to be glad you read it! Yet I cannot be faithful to the truth of God's Word and ignore this reality. There is a Judgment Seat for believers, and each of us will be confronted, one on one, face to face with Jesus Christ. Our eternal success will be clear to us and everyone else at that point.

### Eternal Jewels

What will make it through the fire and come out as gold and precious stones?

- The money we've invested in people, in spreading God's Word, in taking the gospel to every nation, not the money in our bank accounts.
- The service we've rendered to others out of a pure desire to help, to share our plenty with their little, to let God love them through us, not the status we've achieved in the business or the Christian worlds.
- The glory we've passed on to God instead of assuming it for ourselves.
- The people we've influenced to know and serve God, not the people in places of influence that we have known or been.
- The inner clothes of righteousness that we have worn, not the designer clothes in our closets.

- The prisoners, homeless, widows, and orphans we've aided, not the beautifully decorated homes we've bought.
- Everything we've done in the name of Christ and for His glory, not the things we've done in an effort to be seen and appreciated by people.

## The Dangers of the Pursuit of Success

If, then, everything that the world calls success will be meaningless in heaven, should we give everything we own away, resign our positions, and live the rest of our lives in a monastery manner? Is that what it means to look at success with Forever Eyes?

No, there is nothing in Scripture that forbids or condemns career or monetary success. It is possible to be successful in a career or professional pursuit, to receive promotions, to attain high positions, and to excel in our jobs, and be absolutely in line with God's purposes for our lives.

Consider the earthly success enjoyed by many of the heroes and heroines of the Bible. Abraham was a wealthy man in his day. Joseph achieved an extraordinary level of success and power in the secular government of Egypt. Deborah was the Judge of Israel, ruler of all the people. Esther was a queen. David was famous for his military success and his leadership abilities as king of Israel. Solomon was the richest man of his day. The Proverbs 31 woman was successful at home and in business. Among the disciples, Matthew had achieved great monetary success. Lydia was a woman who achieved notable success in a business endeavor. Aquila and Priscilla were successful business owners.

Earthly success does not negate eternal success. Yet the important thing we have to keep remembering is that earthly success does not equal eternal success. Forever Eyes help us to see beyond the trappings of our earthly standards of success and to recognize true greatness in heavenly terms.

## A Model of True Success

There is a man in the Bible who is described as succeeding in everything he undertook (see 2 Chr 32:30b). I'm impressed! What made this man, Hezekiah, such a successful man, and was his success earthly or eternal?

We first meet Hezekiah in 2 Chronicles 28, where we learn that at the age of twenty-five he succeeded his father, Ahaz, as king of Judah and Israel. His father had been very unfaithful to the Lord and had desecrated the altars and temple, and worshiped false gods and idols. Yet the first thing we read about Hezekiah is that he did what was right in the eyes of the Lord, just like David his ancestor.

In spite of an evil father, he had a godly mother, Abijah, daughter of Zechariah, who was one of the last prophets of the Lord, telling of the coming Messiah. In spite of the idolatry of her husband, Abijah remained faithful to the true God and counteracted the evil influence of her husband over her son, Hezekiah.

This should encourage anyone whose parents weren't the people they should have been to know that they are not doomed to follow in their steps. Human psychology sometimes leads people to believe they are victims of their past, but God's Word says differently. No matter what your father or mother was like, you can be a person who pleases the Lord.

## Hezekiah's Secrets of Success

Let me point out some of the main reasons Hezekiah was successful at everything he undertook.

1. First, he cleaned the land of everything that was defiling it.

In the first month he was in office, Hezekiah started repairing the damage done by his godless father. He got rid of the things that were defiling the temple and the people of God. He could never have been successful had he chosen to overlook those things or sweep them under the rug.

2. He gave worship and praise a very high priority in his life and in his land.

After cleaning the temple, Hezekiah called his people to worship. Worship took a very high priority in his life.

3. He was totally obedient to God in every area.

Hezekiah went back to doing things the way God said to do them—no variations, no substitutes. He obeyed God's Word.

4. He encouraged people, and motivated them to do their work with excellence.

Hezekiah spoke encouragingly to his people. He insisted that they do things God's way, but he didn't beat them over the head. He led them by example and by encouraging them.

5. He sought God in everything he did, not trying to do it on his own strength.

Hezekiah didn't succeed all by himself. He was successful because in everything he did, he sought the Lord.

6. He worked very hard and did everything really well.

Hezekiah worked with all his heart, as God showed him what to do.

7. He didn't fold under attack from the enemy, but reaffirmed his faith in God.

Hezekiah had his problems, too, just like us. The enemies of Israel were coming against him, and they were powerful. Hezekiah did everything he could to protect his people against the enemy, then he called them together and said, "Be strong and courageous. Do not be afraid or discouraged because of the king of Assyria and the vast army with him, for there is a greater power with us than with him. With him is only the arm of flesh, but with us is the Lord our God to help us and to fight our battles" (2 Chr 32:7-8a).

Hezekiah didn't fold as soon as the enemy came against him. He confirmed his belief in his God and encouraged his people to believe that greater is He who is in you than he who is in the world.

8. He kept a sensitive ear to God, and repented quickly when God showed him his sin and errors.

Hezekiah had problems with pride, like we all do. He had become very ill, to the point of death, and God had miraculously healed him. Yet his heart was proud and he did not respond to the kindness that the Lord showed him. You'll find this account in 2 Chronicles 32:24-26. We're not given much detail, but I imagine that Hezekiah may have taken the Lord and his deliverance for granted. Or perhaps Hezekiah had had so much success that he was beginning to think it was his power, not God's, that had achieved that success.

Yet as soon as God's wrath was on him and on Judah, as soon as the error of his way was made clear, he "repented of the pride of his heart, as did the people of Jerusalem" (2 Chr 32:26a).

### Follow Hezekiah's Secrets of Success

If we want to have eternal success, to live in such a way that our daily lives are counting for eternity, we would be well advised to follow Hezekiah's example.

*1. Live a pure and clean life and get rid of anything that would hinder purity in your life.*

If you want to know any kind of success, you first have to make your own life clean before God. What idols are there in your life? What things do you treasure more than God? Which people are more important to you than Jesus? Those are idols. You will have to get rid of them, or put them in their proper places in your life, in order to be successful.

*2. Make worship the central theme of your life.*

How much is worship a part of your life? I don't mean just attending church, but rather how much of your own personal time is occupied with worship—praising God, singing, thanking, adoring? It's an absolute essential for success in the life of any Christian.

*3. Obey God's Word to the max!*

It's amazing how few of us really obey God. We rationalize, we procrastinate, and we postpone obedience. One important reason that Hezekiah was successful was that he obeyed.

*4. Become a very good encourager.*

This is a secret of success. In speaking with a friend who was an executive in a local company, I asked how things were going at the office. I knew they'd been struggling with making a profit and cleaning up many things done wrong in the past. My friend, Ray, is a dedicated Christian who was implementing Christian principles as he managed this struggling organization.

He shared with me that they had made their goals the preceding month for the first time in a long time, and he had held a luncheon meeting for all the employees in order to thank them for their efforts in making it happen. He said, "Mary, the people said to me, 'This is the first time we've ever been thanked by this company.'"

Ray was an encourager, just like Hezekiah, and this contributed to the success of Ray's organization. We read in 2 Chronicles 32 that because Hezekiah encouraged his people with words, they gained confidence from what he said. I can guarantee you that it will work that same way in any organization, home, church, or life that practices encouragement.

### 5. Seek God in everything you do.

Do you pray about your job, about your coworkers, about your finances, about your relationships? Do you seek God's will in everything? That's essential in order to be successful.

### 6. Do everything with excellence.

Are you a hard worker, one who goes the extra mile and really gives it all you've got? Colossians 3 says we are to obey our earthly masters with sincerity of heart and reverence for the Lord. Whatever we do, we are to work at it with all our heart, as working for the Lord, not for men.

One of my daily prayers is that I will always do the will of God with excellence, not just so-so, not just OK. Wholehearted work is a foundation of success, whether it's your job or something you do for your family or for a ministry.

*7. Don't fold when the enemy attacks.*

How soon we forget that. We come up against a struggle, a trial, an enemy of some sort, and immediately we give up. Like Hezekiah, we need to believe that our God can defeat all of our enemies. He's greater than any of our problems. If you don't believe this, you'll fail quite frequently.

*8. Keep short accounts with the Lord.*

One of the things I frequently ask God is that He not give me any more success than I'm capable of handling with humility and thankfulness. What I see in so many Christian leaders is that they start with a humble spirit, but with a little success under their belts they let their publicity go to their heads and start believing they've done everything on their own.

One verse I often sing to myself is from the hymn "Come, Thou Fount," which says,

O to grace, how great a debtor
Daily I'm constrained to be!
Let Thy goodness, like a fetter,
Bind my wandering heart to Thee:
Prone to wander, Lord, I feel it,
Prone to leave the God I love;
Here's my heart, O take and seal it;
Seal it for Thy courts above.
(Music by Robert Robins, Words by John Wyeth)

When God has showered his goodness and success on us, we must be sensitive to how easily we can then wander away.

I think Hezekiah's heart started to wander away, but when God showed him that problem, he immediately repented of the pride of his heart and the Lord forgave him and blessed him. What a good lesson to learn from Hezekiah: We'll blow it from time to time, that's for sure, but if we immediately confess, God will forgive and restore.

A life committed to the integrity and holiness of Hezekiah is one headed for eternal success.

### Damaris' Story

My friend Damaris Carbaugh often tells of her pursuit of earthly success. Raised in a wonderful Christian home, she and her two sisters sang as a trio in churches all over the country, traveling with their evangelist mother. At fifteen she was asked to sing at a recording studio, and soon she was in demand by producers and advertising agencies in New York. In the years since, Damaris has sung with many well-known artists in recording sessions. She has performed vocals on countless advertising jingles and commercials for companies like Coca Cola, Pepsi, Kentucky Fried Chicken, Minute Maid, and Wrigley's Chewing Gum.

This taste of the world's success and the money and fame that went with it found a place in her heart. Oh, she fully intended to keep singing for the Lord on Sundays and such, but her heart's greatest desire was to seek a career as a secular performer. In 1982 she won the American Song Festival Talent Search and received a recording contract with CBS Records. She was well on her way to the worldly success she so desired.

However, in 1988 she visited a group of believers in Argentina who live in abject poverty. She was struck by their devotion to the Lord in spite of their circumstances, serving Him not for His blessings but for the pure joy of loving Him. God used this to give Damaris some Forever Eyes, and she began to see how empty and worthless worldly success was. She began to desire to give herself totally to the Lord, and began praying for ways to use her talents more fully for Him.

God has opened many avenues of service for Damaris since then, as she sings with the Brooklyn Tabernacle Choir, the "Day of Discovery" television program, and in her own solo concerts and appearances. She is one of the few successful Christian artists who has no agent, no large fee requirements, no "entourage." She does not see herself as a diva or a professional singer, but as a servant of the Living God.

Forever Eyes change our idea of success, and this sets us free from the driving ambitions of this world and the need to achieve some earthly plateau in order to prove our worth. For some of us, it is difficult to let go of those success dreams, but to do so is to find life abundant in the good work that the Lord Jesus has planned for us.

## Six

# Looking at Difficulties With *Forever* Eyes

Like many in our generation, my brothers and I are in the stage of life where we are the caretakers of our mother. Dad died in 1999 after sixty-four years of marriage to my mom. Since then we've had no choice but to situate my mom in a nursing home near my brother, as she requires twenty-four-hour care.

I have struggled with the ending to my mother's life perhaps more than with anything else that has ever happened to me personally. Let me change that sentence: I am struggling with it. You see, my mom is the godliest woman I have ever known, and because she loved God's Word so much and studied it so faithfully and taught it so well for so many years, I always thought that she would never have mental disabilities. I remember saying, perhaps with some pride, that Mom would never have to battle senility, because her mind was fortified so thoroughly with God's Word.

Yet I was wrong. Her mind is a battlefield of jumbled memories, scrambled imaginations, and instant forgetfulness, and her quality of life is poor. This mental disability has caused her to be immobile and totally dependent on others for every need.

As I pray for her, I fight the anger and sadness that wells up inside of me. Why, God? If she couldn't end her life in a more dignified way, why have you allowed her to continue on in this manner? I hear of others who have parents as old or older than she is, who are still caring for themselves, living in their homes, enjoying their lives, and I struggle against envy. I daydream about being able to bring my mom to visit me, taking her on a trip with me, having her come hear me speak, as she and Dad did so many times. I think of how wonderful her last years could have been if only her mind had remained strong.

How do you live with a sickness or infirmity that is unexplainable? How do you come to a place of acceptance, understanding, or peace when you or someone you love is caught in the web of a disabled or diseased body or an infirm mind?

As I have struggled to see my mom's condition through Forever Eyes, I have found some solace. With much effort, against my feelings, I have forced myself to look beyond the here and now, which certainly seems awfully long right now, and to recognize that in eternity this will seem trivial. In eternity my mother will be the first one to say, "What matter that those last years were less than I would have liked? They are nothing in comparison to an eternity with the Lord."

I have dear friends in my church who are facing a much more serious health issue, because Craig is only fifty years old, and the doctors have said that he will probably live only two to four more years with his current cancer. I am in awe at Craig's and Marion's ability to accept this illness from God's hands. I can see how God is using even this terrible prognosis to touch lives as Craig and Marion share with so many people the peace that God has given them.

OK, I might be able to look through Forever Eyes and say, "Well, people are coming to saving faith because of Craig's illness, and from an eternal viewpoint, that balances the scales." I know that Craig and Marion see it that way. Yet why does a ninety-year-old woman have to spend her last years in such a state that she is not even able to articulate her faith?

"Lord, give me Forever Eyes," I pray, as I think about Mom. And

His Spirit assures me that things are going on of which I have no knowledge and won't until eternity. I'm looking at the outward appearances, and God sees so much more than I do. I think of the people in Mom's home who are with her each day, and who often say to me, "She's the sweetest lady I've ever met," and God reminds me that He can use us as witnesses to His grace, even in demented stages of life.

I think of how Mom can still quote much of the Scripture she memorized through the years, even though she can't remember what she had for breakfast, and how her eyes light up as she stutters through those familiar passages. I think of the testimony she is to her grandchildren and great-grandchildren, even in her current condition, and I see how God takes our suffering and transforms it into blessing.

## Transformed Suffering

There are so many examples throughout the history of the church of people who have been dealt a terrible physical blow, and yet that very condition has given them a voice for God that they would never have had otherwise. Amy Carmichael served in India, ministering to the worst of society for fifty-six years without a furlough. The last twenty years of her life she was an invalid because of a freak accident. She stepped in a hole, and her back and legs were never the same. Her suffering is now for us an encouragement of God's faithfulness.

Joni Erickson Tada is a present-day reminder that God transforms suffering into His glory, and I've heard her say that she would not change the circumstances of her life even if she could, because as a quadriplegic, she has known God and God has used her in powerful ways. Amy and Joni have looked at their suffering through Forever Eyes and never looked back.

The apostle Paul left us the ultimate example of looking at suffering through Forever Eyes when he faced a debilitating disability. He called it a "thorn in my flesh" and referred to it as a "messenger of Satan, to torment me" (2 Cor 12:7). Three times he pleaded with the Lord to take it away from him. Note that this suffering was not from God, but rather from Satan. It would seem logical to our minds that God's answer to Paul's prayer would be to take away the torment that the enemy had inflicted upon Paul.

However, Paul tells us how God responded to his threefold plea:

> *But he said to me, "My grace is sufficient for you, for my power is made perfect in weakness." Therefore I will boast all the more gladly about my weaknesses, so that Christ's power may rest on me. That is why, for Christ's sake, I delight in weaknesses, in insults, in hardships, in persecutions, in difficulties. For when I am weak, then I am strong.*

2 CORINTHIANS 12:9-10

When we study the life of the apostle Paul, we are tempted to think that he lived on a different planet than the rest of us. He is universally recognized as, if not *the* greatest, then one of the greatest disciples of Jesus Christ. Yet dealing with this "thorn in the flesh" was no easier for him than it would be for us. He pleaded with God three times to take it away. This didn't come easy for him.

He was able to arrive at a place of acceptance because he could look beyond the current suffering to see the eternal purpose. He saw his suffering through Forever Eyes.

Perhaps our generation finds this more difficult because we have so many more medical remedies and resources than were available in Paul's time. We are accustomed to having a pill to kill a headache, a capsule to destroy an infection, an injection to immunize against disease. Enduring suffering is not in our life experience, and it seems cruel and absurd to suggest that it could be God's will.

In his book, *The Hidden Smile of God*, John Piper addresses this topic. The subtitle to his book is "The Fruit of Affliction in the Lives of John Bunyan, William Cowper, and David Brainerd." Mr. Piper introduces us to three great men of our faith who suffered greatly in different ways.

Bunyan suffered unjust treatment and spent years in prison because of his faith, but that confinement led to *The Pilgrim's Progress*, one of the classics of Christian literature. This is a book that has influenced thousands and thousands of people through the centuries.

William Cowper wrote some of the great hymns of our church, words that are awesome in their praise and glory of God. Perhaps most famous is "God Moves in a Mysterious Way." Here are two of its very profound verses:

God moves in a mysterious way,
His wonders to perform;
He plants his footsteps in the sea,
And rides upon the storm.


Ye fearful saints, fresh courage take,
The clouds ye so much dread
Are big with mercy, and shall break
In blessings on your head.


Yet Cowper, this poet of rare beauty and eloquence, suffered greatly with mental anguish and deep depression through all his years.

David Brainerd was a missionary to the Indians in America in the early years of our country, and he died at a very early twenty-nine years of age. Yet his dedication to serve the Lord in spite of constant sickness—incurable consumption, as it was diagnosed in his day—and the writings in his journal have challenged and encouraged more people to a life of missionary work than perhaps any other single person.

John Piper writes:

> Oh, how we need Bunyan! We are soft and thin-skinned. We are worldly; we fit far too well into our God-ignoring culture. We are fearful and anxious and easily discouraged. We have taken our eyes off the Celestial City and the deep pleasures of knowing God and denying ourselves the lesser things that titillate for a moment but then shrink our capacities for great joy.[1]

In *The Pilgrim's Progress*, Pilgrim is headed to the Celestial City, and he makes his way through many difficulties and struggles by keeping his eye on that eternal city. I fear there are many Christians today who have never read this classic, may never even have heard of it. If you, dear reader, are one of these, please put it at the top of your reading list. The imagery will make its way into your mind and give you inestimable aid in remembering to look at your life through Forever Eyes—to keep looking at the Celestial City.

In Hebrews 13:12-14 (RSV) we find these words:

> *Jesus also suffered outside the gate in order to sanctify the people through his own blood. Therefore let us go forth to him outside the camp, and bearing abuse for him. For here we have no lasting city, but we seek the city which is to come.*

Referring to Brainerd, Piper writes:

> When you spend the last seven years of your life spitting up blood and die at age twenty-nine, you don't just say those words—"here we have no lasting city"—you feel them the way you feel the wind on a cliff's edge. Oh, how many feel the wind and run inland! The call of Christ and the call of Brainerd are exactly the opposite of such a retreat: Since we have no lasting city here, stop working so hard trying to make it lasting and luxurious, and "go forth to him outside the camp"—outside the safe place, outside the comfortable place.[2]

I confess that I have not arrived at Brainerd's place, or Bunyan's or Cowper's. My experience is quite different and I may never be called on to suffer in those ways. Yet Piper's words still apply to me and can make a huge difference in my life, if I will but learn from these great men. I need to stop working so hard trying to make this temporary homesite lasting and luxurious.

## Looking at the Unseen

Most people know that "Joshua fit the battle of Jericho and the walls came tumblin' down!" It seems to me, however, that all too often we read these accounts of old in Scripture and never stop to realize that these people were not superhumans. They were quite like us in their humanness, and before those walls came tumblin' down, Joshua had to see them down.

*Then the Lord said to Joshua, "See, I have delivered Jericho into your hands, along with its king and its fighting men. March around the city once with all the armed men. Do this for six days. Have seven priests carry trumpets of rams' horns in front of the ark. On the seventh day, march around the city seven times, with the priests blowing the trumpets. When you hear them sound a long blast on the trumpets, have all the people give a loud shout; then the wall of the city will collapse and the people will go up, every man straight in."*

JOSHUA 6:2-5

Please notice verse 2: "See, I have delivered Jericho into your hands...." See?! See what? Can you imagine what your reaction would have been if the Lord had said to you, "See, I have delivered Jericho into your hands," and as yet there were immense and thick walls between you and Jericho? If you looked at Jericho then, what would you see? What did Joshua see with his earthly eyes? Walls! Yet the Lord Himself told Joshua to see that those walls were gone, and Jericho was defeated.

One of the most dangerous teachings of the New Age movement has been the idea of visualization. They teach that if you will simply visualize the result you desire, then that result will happen. The power for this, they say, is found within yourself, in your ability to visualize what you want to happen.

I would point out that this New Age visualization teaching is a corruption of a biblical principle that we need to learn to practice. We need to see the difficulties in our lives as God sees them, and recognize that our walls are nothing more than God's opportunities.

The difference between Forever Eyes and New Age teaching is that with Forever Eyes we see what God wants to do and can do. We see beyond the difficulties and believe that God can take down the walls that stand between us and what He has planned for us.

It's important to understand that Jericho's walls came down because that was God's plan, not Joshua's. God intended to give Joshua's people that land, and the walls were absolutely useless against God's plans. So, we are not talking about a "name it/claim it" type of faith, where anything your heart desires can be yours if you can visualize it and claim it. However, if God intends to bring the walls down, you certainly can see them as down.

Difficulties, pain, affliction—all of these are a part of our lives. How we see them is up to us. Psalm 119:67 says, "Before I was afflicted I went astray, but now I obey your word." That is true in my own life. My affliction was self-imposed; I went astray knowing full well that I was headed in the wrong direction, but determined to run my life the way I wanted it. That led me to affliction. I brought pain and suffering on myself and my family, and dishonored the name of Christ.

I could have learned my lessons in a much less painful way, but how few of us ever do. Before I was afflicted I went astray, but now I obey God's word. That affliction taught me how painful, dreary, and unsatisfying my way is. Since I seem to be a slow learner, perhaps this was the only way I could have ever really learned that lesson.

At any rate, I can now thank God for the ten years of misery, as I tried to find a way to feel good about myself. The sleepless nights, the frantic pace, even the deteriorated lifestyle—all of these brought me finally to the end of myself, and I now obey His word. Those ten years take on eternal significance, even with all my regrets, because I can look at them through Forever Eyes.

## Kerri's Story

I have asked my friend Kerri if I could share her story with you, because it is a wonderful illustration of learning to look at difficulties with Forever Eyes. She tells it in her own words.

\*\*\*\*\*

I can't remember a time that I didn't know the name of Jesus. I know that this is an incredible blessing to be raised in a home where my parents loved and served the Lord. In fact, my dad was a minister, so church was like our second home.

One day, when I was almost five years old, I realized as I sat in Sunday school that I wasn't going to heaven. The next day I went to find my mom so I could ask more about this. I found her washing my sister's hair in the bathroom. I asked questions, and when my sister's hair was done I sat down, right there in the bathroom, and asked Jesus to forgive me for my sins, and I invited Him to come into my heart to live. All these years I can see that Jesus has been with me. I'm glad He is my Savior.

Soon after the commitment to follow Jesus, my life would change. My faith, even though that of a child, would be tested. The unthinkable would happen. I got sick. After I complained of a stomachache, we went to the doctor and a lump was found. I had cancer. We were soon to find out that this cancer was stage four, or to put it plainly, the worst it could be. The prognosis was poor.

People began to pray. Our family, our friends, our church, and people I didn't even know, from other churches, prayed for me.

And where was God? He was with me when I was alone in the hospital during the three surgeries I had. He was there with me through all the radiation treatments. He was there with me during each painful search to find a vein in order to give me chemo. He was with me when that same chemo made me very sick and caused my hair to fall out. He gave me strength to go to school with a wig.

After two years the cancer was gone and the doctor told my parents, "I can give you many reasons why your daughter shouldn't be here; I can't give you one why she is." We knew the reason was God. He chose to heal me, and through the process He taught me that He is always with me.

When God does an incredible miracle in your life, He also gives you a faith that He will always be there. I knew that not only was God real, He really cared about me. For some reason He chose to spare my life, and I was so thankful. I'm glad He was my Healer.

I praise Him for healing me. But I also praise Him for another part of my life. A part of my life that was very painful. A part of my life that I wouldn't have chosen.

I lost a dream through my cancer. It took several years to realize that the dream was shattered, and I found myself confronted with a different side of God than what I had known. I had known God as a God of miracles in my life, but now I was facing a great disappointment, and I found that there was much more to learn about who God is.

Throughout my childhood my sister and I best loved to pretend to be mommies. I believe that is where my dream began. I wanted to be a mom. What I learned after I was married, however, was that because of the kind of cancer I had had, it was unlikely that I would be able to have a child.

I had never felt such sorrow. I learned three words during this time: barren, hope, and surrender.

"Barren" is not a very nice word, is it? Yet there is something about that word with which I can identify. The imagery of the desert, empty, lonely, barren—that was the way my heart felt. Even now when I say the word I feel it hit like a weight in the bottom of my stomach with its stark reality. That's what it is. Reality. My reality. I am barren, and I feel barren—dry, empty, dead inside. I am barren, and it hurts.

Facing infertility was a grieving process, a mourning of the children I would never have. In a song by Wes King he describes it as missing someone you have never met. If there had been a funeral then not only would I have had the opportunity for closure but people would have known the depth of my pain. Even I was often surprised by the depth of my sorrow and despair. It would surface at odd times. Seeing a baby in the grocery line or watching a diaper commercial could send me into a sobbing fit. I felt sometimes that I had no control of my emotions. I hated Mother's Day. I couldn't go to baby showers. When my friends began having babies I had a hard time being excited for them.

People would often ask innocent questions that were painful. "When are you going to start a family?" If I didn't want to go into the whole explanation I would just say, "When God gives us a child." I was hoping that God would give us a child.

This brings me to the next word: hope. Surprisingly, "hope" became a painful word for me. I believed that God could heal me. The doctors said there was less than a 1 percent chance that I would have a baby. Funny that hope can withstand those odds. Hope grabs onto the smallest chance. At times I wished the doctor had said there was no chance, no way, no how, that I could have a child. Yet, isn't that really what he said—less than 1 percent? That is as close to zero as you can get, but when you combine it with faith in a God of miracles, anything can happen, right?

It was a good hope, wasn't it, to hope for a child? So I asked, begged, pleaded with God to answer my prayer, and I had hope that my dream would come true. Each month I faced the disappointment when it didn't happen. Hope began to torture me. Eventually I had to face the possibility that God was saying no. What do you do with that? But God, why? Why can't we have a child? Why? You can do it, I know You can—why won't You? I knew the reality of deep, desperate pain.

As time went by I didn't know what to pray. Was it all right for me to pray for a miracle? In one of those times of sorrow, I asked my husband what I should pray. He said to pray what Jesus prayed, when He was in sorrow. You remember, at Gethsemane: "Abba, Father, everything is possible for you. Take this cup from me. Yet not what I will, but what you will" (Mk 14:36). That opened my eyes. First, I realized that Jesus knew how I felt. He had faced sorrow way beyond what I was facing. Second, He showed me how to deal with my desire. I could ask God to work the miracle, but I had to entrust the answer to Him.

That brings us to my third word: Surrender. I'd like to tell you that I just prayed a prayer of surrender and that was it. Yet surrender was a process for me—a three-steps-forward-two-steps-back process. It was hard to see any progress. It was often hard to see beyond the pain. Unfortunately, there was no way around it. I had to go through it. And as I inched along, year after year, I began to realize that it was getting better. I began to accept this plan God had and began to let go of my own. He changed my desire from a hope to bear children to a hope in His perfect plan for me, whatever that might be.

The thing about surrender is that God takes your willing heart and He fills it with the desire to do His will, His good and perfect will. You know, I gave it to Him kicking and screaming all the way and yet for some reason He chose to bless us beyond our wildest dreams.

No, I didn't get pregnant. I am still a barren woman, but God filled my arms. He chose a different way for us. He picked out a little boy in Guatemala to be our son.

Do you know that after I held our little Luke in my arms I was actually glad I was barren? It is unbelievable to say that, but if I could have borne my own children I might never have received this blessing from God. Isn't our God good? He doesn't make life blissfully happy for us. He cares about our character too much. He reveals Himself through the trials we face, and through them He blesses us more than we can imagine.

I hope my life is a testimony to our awesome God. He is our Savior, Healer, Lord, and so much more. Look and you will see Him all around you, working out His will, His good and perfect will. He will never leave you or forsake you. You can entrust Him with everything, even that desire that you hold so tightly. Surrender it to Him and you will be surprised at His blessings.

## Seven

# Looking at Time
# With *Forever* Eyes

All of us, everyone reading this book and everyone you know, will live forever. How do I know? Because God's Word teaches us this truth. We will live a certain number of days on this earth, and then each of us will transition into the life hereafter, and that life never ends! *Never!*

The Bible clearly teaches that there are two places where people will spend their hereafter lives—heaven and hell. Those are the only options we have, and before we leave this life, our decision about Jesus Christ determines whether we will transition from this life into heaven or into hell.

This afterlife in heaven or hell is endless. Our brains blow a fuse as we try to imagine numberless days, but of course, that is what eternity is—numberless days in heaven or hell. The days before the afterlife we call time, and we are constantly reminded that we run on time. Our lives are full of reminders: clocks, timetables, schedules, itineraries, and deadlines, to name a few.

### Numbered Days

The days here on earth are numbered for each of us, and each of us has a different number. We just don't know what that number is.

Furthermore, we have only limited control, at best, over that number. So, we live with continual uncertainty, knowing for sure that we have limited, numbered days, but not knowing how many.

Most of us tend to live as though these earthly days are going to go on for a very long time. Typically, the younger we are, the more we ignore, dismiss, or refuse to believe that our days are numbered. Children and teenagers never seem to grasp the reality that their days are numbered. As we grow older, we become more aware of our limited time here on this earth. Yet even then, few of us truly live as though our days are numbered.

I recently met a woman who told me that her father has lung cancer because of his smoking habit. The doctor has told him that if he continues to smoke, he most surely will die very soon. Yet he refuses to quit smoking, and in fact denies that smoking has caused his cancer! He will not face the fact that his days are numbered—and they are few.

David wrote:

*You have made my days a mere handbreadth; the span of my years is as nothing before you. Each man's life is but a breath.*

PSALM 39:5

And again:

*As for man, his days are like grass, he flourishes like a flower of the field; the wind blows over it and it is gone, and its place remembers it no more.*

PSALM 103:15-16

These verses shock our souls. They don't bring us great comfort, as a rule, and we're not prone to meditate on them for very long. Who wants to think of his or her life as a mere breath of air, a flower that quickly flourishes? Surely we are more significant than that! Surely someone will remember us when we are gone!

Yet the message for us here is not that these earthly days are unimportant, but that eternity is far greater. David saw his days on this earth as inconsequential because he compared earthly days to eternal, numberless days. He looked at his time with Forever Eyes.

Given the fact that we are all going to live forever, and assuming that most of us have made a decision to accept Christ into our lives, which means we know we will transition from this earthly life to life with God in heaven, then we need to have the right perspective of our days on earth, do we not?

David wrote:

> *Show me, O Lord, my life's end and the number of my days; let me know how fleeting is my life.*
>
> PSALM 39:4

And Moses prayed:

> *Teach us to number our days aright, that we may gain a heart of wisdom.*
>
> PSALM 90:12

Moses is not telling us to number the days gone by; we all know what that number is, and some of us can't believe it's as big as it is! He is asking God to teach us to number the days we have left here before we transition into the life hereafter, where we will have endless days. He is asking Him to teach us to remember that no matter what the number is, it is inconsequential compared to endless days.

## Living in Numbered Days

We need to live every day in the knowledge of how fleeting these earthly days are, no matter how many more of them we may have. This is a lesson for us to learn—Moses asked God to "teach us," indicating that we don't know how to do this naturally. It doesn't come easy for us. We have to learn to number our days aright.

Our natural tendency is to be focused on the earth days left to us— even though we have no idea how many there are. We spend our time and our energy, we set our priorities and make decisions based on the days we have on this earth—or the days we think we have on this earth—as though they were far more important than anything else.

When we learn to number our days aright, we will look at these earthly days very differently, because in comparison to eternity, they are far less significant. We'll make decisions differently; our priorities will change; we'll spend our money differently; and we'll use our time more wisely.

How can we learn to number our days aright? Keeping the Judgment Seat of Christ in our minds on a daily basis will help us to do this, as we discussed in chapter five. It will affect how we use our time, how much time we waste, what we make a priority in our lives, and what we learn to say "no" to.

## Number Your Days

If you live to be very old and die of old age, how many more years do you have on this earth? Pick a number. It could be seventy, fifty, twenty, or ten. Be generous and pick a large number. Write it here:

At best I figure I have _____ more years to live on this earth.

Now, compare that number to one hundred. Which is larger?

Compare that number to one thousand. Which is larger?

Compare that number to one million. Which is larger?

Where will you be in one hundred years? Where will you be in one thousand years? Where will you be in one million years? We will all be in eternity, and if you have been born from above, you will be in eternity with the Lord Jesus Christ.

Let's try to make a side-by-side comparison:

| Years left to live | compared to | Eternity |
|---|---|---|
| 10 | | Numberless |
| 20 | | Numberless |
| 30 | | Numberless |
| 40 | | Numberless |
| 50 | | Numberless |
| 60 | | Numberless |
| 70 | | Numberless |
| 80 | | Numberless |

The illustration seems ridiculous—any number you can name is insignificant compared to eternity. There is no ending to eternity, and in God's heaven it will be an eternity of peace, perfection, and joy. Try to imagine life without end; it blows the fuses of your mind.

Once again, take the number you wrote down, your best guess at the ideal number of years you have left here on this earth before beginning your eternal years, and ask yourself what your dreams are for those remaining years. Dream your best dreams and imagine them all coming true.

Then ask yourself, will they make it to eternity? Am I living my life now in the light of eternity, or is my sight limited to the end of my days?

Undoubtedly one of the reasons David was a man after God's own heart was because he could see beyond his earthly days. He looked with Forever Eyes, and reminded us that whatever number of days are left to us here, they are nothing compared to eternity.

> *Man is a mere phantom as he goes to and fro: He bustles about, but only in vain; he heaps up wealth, not knowing who will get it.*
> PSALM 39:6

What an accurate picture David gives us of the typical person—even the typical Christian—in today's world. Many of us are spending our time in pursuit of things that will go into someone else's hands. They won't make it to eternity.

## Messages From the Person You Will Be

I recently caught one line from a television commercial that was advertising the benefits of a health-related product. The commercial began with this question: "If the woman you will be in twenty years could talk to the woman you are now, what would she say to you?" The first half of that question caused me to stop and quickly write it down.

The woman I will be in twenty years will be older and wiser. She will have a perspective that I do not now have. Would she have some of these messages for me?

- You're wasting valuable time on many things that do not matter.
- You're missing opportunities for service to God that will never come your way again.

- You're throwing away energy and resources on things that will burn up.
- You're living as though your days are numberless; they are not.

My guess is that the woman I will be in twenty years would take the woman I am today by the collar and try to shake some sense into my head, try to peel off the blinders that keep me immersed in the here and now. The woman I will be in twenty years would remind me that time is short, twenty years pass quickly, and time is my most valuable asset. It can never be replaced. Once you spend it, it is gone forever. The woman I will be in twenty years would beg me to live every day of my life with Forever Eyes.

The woman I will be in twenty years would ask, "What difference will what you are doing today make in twenty years?" It could be that the woman I will be in twenty years will already be in eternity, and she would ask, "What difference will what you are doing today make in eternity?"

Living our lives in the light of eternity is dramatically life changing because it motivates us to be good stewards of the minutes and hours that we have left. Recognizing that we don't know how many days we have left, we live every day as though it could be the last. Our time management skills greatly improve. Our irritation over inconsequential issues is eliminated. Our concern over matters that don't matter goes away.

Living now in the light of eternity brings freedom, joy, and contentment that we'll never know otherwise. It is the gateway to a meaningful, intentional lifestyle, full of challenges and even some sorrows, but never trite, never inconsequential. What are we waiting for?

### Eight

# Looking at Money and Possessions With *Forever* Eyes

My daddy used to say to my brothers and me, "Money just burns a hole in your pockets!" Having been raised during the Depression years, he and my mother were very frugal, and the two of them stretched Dad's slim paycheck an incredibly long way. They tried to teach their three children the same attitude toward money.

Never having had to face Depression days as they did, I'm not nearly the frugal person they were. Money does still "burn holes in my pockets," so to speak. Truth be known, I rarely deny myself anything I truly want. Yet whether you are a frugal person or not, money can still be a major issue in your life, because money can burn a hole in your heart.

Did you know that the Bible has more than two thousand verses about money? In fact, there is more ink in the Bible about money and possessions than there is about heaven. This tells me that God considers money and the things it can buy a very important topic.

## Money's Bid for Control

Jesus fully understood the power of money and its ability to quickly and easily make its way to the throne of our hearts. He said, "No one can serve two masters. Either he will hate the one and love the other, or he will be devoted to the one and despise the other. You cannot serve both God and Money" (Mt 6:24).

Let me quote from Richard Foster's book, *The Challenge of the Disciplined Life: Christian Reflections on Money, Sex, and Power:*

> Money has power, spiritual power, to win our hearts.... Mammon asks for our allegiance in a way that sucks the milk of human kindness out of our very being.... And in point of fact, money has many of the characteristics of deity. It gives us security, can induce guilt, gives us freedom, gives us power and seems to be omnipresent. Most sinister of all, however, is its bid for omnipotence.[1]

"Its bid for omnipotence"—that means money can easily become the master of our lives, the power to which we are in slavery, in bondage. It can burn a hole in your heart that leaves little room for anything else.

No wonder Jesus said, "You cannot serve both God and Money." They are rivals, opposed to each other, both seeking our loyalty and commitment. And one of them will win; one of them is winning. If you had to state which one was winning in your heart right now, today, which one would it be?

### Love-of-Money Griefs

Paul wrote to young Timothy, "For the love of money is a root of all kinds of evil. Some people, eager for money, have wandered from the faith and pierced themselves with many griefs" (1 Tm 6:10).

Self-inflicted griefs are often caused by the love of money. Think of some of these love-of-money griefs:

**Broken or Damaged Relationships**

"Never loan money to a friend" is an old adage with some good advice. Once money becomes an issue in a friendship, the damage can be irreparable.

Counselors tell us that one of the major causes of marriage breakups is money. Certainly one of the major causes of arguments and disagreements among married couples is money.

**Dishonesty and Deception**

When money is at stake, how easy it is to lie or deceive. Some years ago, when I was working as a business trainer, I allowed a situation to develop that went against the agreement I had with the training company for whom I worked as a freelance trainer. Basically, I recognized an opportunity to make extra money by skirting the rules and dealing directly with a client instead of working through the training organization. I thought of how I needed the money, I rationalized that everyone else did it all the time, and I allowed it to happen. Wouldn't you know, it got back to the training company, and I was held to account for it.

I remember the phone call I placed to the manager of the training company, with apologies and regrets. This woman had thought of me as a person with the highest integrity; she knew my commitment as a Christian. Now I had to admit to her that I had been deceptive, had broken the rules knowingly, all for a little bit of money! Money had caused me to do something I normally would never have thought of doing. A self-inflicted grief, for sure!

**Workaholism**

No doubt there are many reasons people become workaholics, but money would rank up there toward the top, I suspect. Like other addictions, the effects of workaholism are felt by more than just the workaholic. They spill over to family members and friends, and they affect physical health and mental attitude.

These are just a few of the self-inflicted griefs that can be avoided if money is seen with Forever Eyes, if it isn't allowed to burn a hole in your heart.

## The Smell of Money's Control

Here are some of the telltale signs that money has burned a hole in your heart:

- Money causes you a great deal of fear and anxiety.
- You find yourself dreaming about somehow coming into a lot of money, and the things you'd do with it.
- You envy people who seem to have all the money they need.
- You think of money as the solution to all your problems.
- You look to money for security.
- You evaluate people by their financial success.

Just imagine that overnight for some horrible reason you were left devoid of all financial security. Your bank accounts, your retirement funds, your savings, your jewelry, your real estate—everything you own that has value was just wiped out. Would you be ready to commit suicide? Would you feel that life was over? Would you go crazy?

I often make myself think through this scenario, as a way of evaluating where I am in my attitude toward money. If I'm honest, it's a very telling exercise, because it makes me see how much I treasure my possessions, and where my treasure is, there is my heart, my commitment, my devotion.

I was amazed to read this account of the Hebrew Christians:

*You sympathized with those in prison and joyfully accepted the confiscation of your property, because you knew that you yourselves had better and lasting possessions.*

HEBREWS 10:34

"Joyfully accepted the confiscation of your property"—imagine! The members of this group of believers certainly were looking with Forever Eyes, to be able not just to endure but to joyfully accept the loss of all their property. I would love to have been there and witnessed that event. I wonder how those who were confiscating their property reacted to their joyful acceptance. What a testimony that must have been.

How could they do it? Because they looked beyond the here and now and fully believed that their eternal possessions were better, and nobody could confiscate those. They were in heaven, where moths and rust could not corrupt them, and where thieves could not steal them (see Mt 6:20). This was better than being federally insured, wouldn't you agree?

When Jesus told us we could not serve both God and money, he personified money as a rival god. He made it clear that money is not morally neutral; it is a power that seeks to dominate us. It is capable of inspiring devotion, and all we have to do is read our newspapers to see what horrible things people do because of the control money has over them.

As Foster points out in his book, money asks for our allegiance in a way that sucks the milk of human kindness out of our very being. It seems that money is not willing to rest contented in its proper place alongside other things we value. No, it yells for supremacy, and we attach importance to it far beyond its value.

Think of the rich young ruler who came to Jesus wanting to know what he must do to have eternal life. Jesus nailed him on the thing in his life to which he was a slave: his money. Jesus said, "If you want to be perfect, go, sell your possessions and give to the poor, and you will have treasure in heaven. Then come, follow me" (Mt 19:21). Yet the young man went away sad. He wanted to obey Jesus. He wanted eternal life, but he was so enslaved to his money that he couldn't make the break.

Now, just think about what must have happened to this rich young ruler, unless he changed his mind at some later point in his life. He was undoubtedly physically comfortable for the rest of his earthly life, with all the power and trappings of wealth around him. Yet eventually he died, and he now faces an eternity without Christ.

I wonder what that young ruler would say to us now if he were here. Don't you imagine that eternity has changed his perspective tremendously? Do you think he'd be willing to sell all his possessions now, if he could have another chance?

## Rejecting the Lordship of Money

Jesus makes it clear that in order to be His disciple, we must knowingly and consciously reject money as a god in our lives. Let me ask you: Have you ever consciously rejected money as a god in your life? Do you on a regular basis confirm to God and to yourself that money is not your master, and that you intend to reject it as a controlling force over you?

If you've never done this, I want to encourage you to give it strong consideration, because the power of money will cause most of us to become its servant if we do not overtly and repeatedly refuse to allow it to control us.

I never thought of myself as money-hungry, but the more deeply I dig into my fears and motivation, the more I realize that money has burned a hole in my heart. It takes constant vigilance and prayer to keep it from crawling onto the altar of my heart and becoming my master.

One of the things I pray frequently is that God will make me "possessionless"—Richard Foster's term. By that I mean that He will cause me to realize that I truly do not possess anything. I am simply a steward of God's possessions; His name is on the owner's certificate, not mine.

On a regular basis I mentally hold up to God the money in my bank account, the home I live in, my income, the things I have that would be listed as an asset. I say to God, "These are not mine, they are Yours. You have loaned them to me, but I do not own them. I simply recognize what is the truth: I am possessionless."

If I don't do this on a regular basis, very easily what I think I own starts to own me, and I become possessed by my possessions. I encourage you to make a habit of renouncing the ownership of whatever it is you think you possess.

A very powerful way to make certain that money does not control us is to give it away. Let me quote from Foster's book:

> Without question, money has taken on a sacred character in our world, and it would do us good to find ways to defame it, defile it, and trample it under our feet. So step on it. Yell at it. Laugh at it. List it way down on the scale of values.... And engage in the most profane act of all—give it away. The powers that energize money cannot abide that most unnatural of acts, giving. Money is made for taking, for bargaining, for manipulating, but not for giving. This is exactly why giving has such ability to defeat the powers of money.[2]

Remember that in eternity, how much money you make, how much you have saved, how prosperous you have been, how many things you own will count for absolutely nothing. These things will be worthless in eternity, unless you've used what God has entrusted to you for eternal purposes.

## Possessing or Possessed?

In Luke 12:15 Jesus warns us again about being possessed by our possessions: "Watch out! Be on your guard against all kinds of greed; a man's life does not consist in the abundance of his possessions." Certainly possessing money—even lots of it—is not wrong or sinful. There are people who have been blessed with large fortunes and have used their fortunes for eternal good. God can trust a few people to do that.

Yet, quite frankly, not many of us would be trustworthy with a large fortune. It would change us for the worse; it would adversely affect our relationships; it would distract us from higher priorities.

If we "count our days," compared to eternity, the amount of money we may accumulate here on earth is pretty unimportant. It won't impress God, and if it is not spent for eternal purposes, it will burn up at the Judgment Seat. When you count your days, money looks quite different.

Please note this passage from 2 Peter 3:

*But the day of the Lord will come like a thief. The heavens will disappear with a roar; the elements will be destroyed by fire, and the earth and everything in it will be laid bare.*

*Since everything will be destroyed in this way, what kind of*

*people ought you to be? You ought to live holy and godly lives as you*
*look forward to the day of God and speed its coming.*

2 PETER 3:10-12a

### Your Heavenly Audit

Living holy and godly lives is never a function of earthly riches. You may be quite humble in earthly goods—even poor—and be very wealthy in eternity's view. If you are sending treasures ahead of you to heaven, your bank account there may be overflowing, even though you live from paycheck to paycheck here on earth.

My friend Judy would fit that description. She commutes to Chicago each day on the train, and makes it her mission to give away three Bibles every day. She prays that God will direct her to the appropriate people, and with His guidance, she sows the Word of God in the lives of three people each workday. These are people she will most likely never see again here on earth. I wonder how many of them will greet her in heaven and thank her for the Word of Life she gave them.

I don't think Judy has accumulated much of this world's wealth. She doesn't own a car, and lives in a nice but simple rental apartment. Sometimes she has to "pray in" the money she needs to buy the Bibles she gives away! Yet she is rich toward God because she looks at earthly money and possessions with Forever Eyes. Her heavenly audit will reveal her true wealth.

Imagine a heavenly auditor assessing your wealth right now—your heavenly wealth. How much have you sent on ahead of you? Do you have more earthly assets than heavenly ones? Remember, the earthly ones won't be in heaven. They will be of no value in eternity, unless you use them for eternal purposes. Jesus said, "What is highly valued among men is detestable in God's sight" (Lk 16:15b).

These words convict me even as I write them. I wonder how embarrassed I would be if I had a heavenly audit right now? Imagine how much worse that will be at the Judgment Seat of Christ when we will give an account of our stewardship.

On the other hand, isn't it a great relief to know that your earthly assets may be few, but your heavenly assets can be many? Jesus told the disciples that it was more difficult for a camel to pass through the eye of a needle than it was for a rich person to enter the kingdom of God (see Mt 19:24; Mk 10:25; Lk 18:25). That's because earthly riches are almost always a distraction from eternal values.

Looking at money and possessions with Forever Eyes will be a continual challenge for most of us. Yet we can do it if we really want to, and if we even begin to see them through God's eyes.

### The Dishonest Shrewd Manager

Jesus told a very strange parable in Luke 16:1-9 about a manager who was wasting his master's possessions. He was an unsatisfactory employee, and his appraisal went like this:

> *So he [the master] called him in and asked him, "What is this I hear about you? Give an account of your management, because you cannot be manager any longer."*
>
> LUKE 16:2

He was fired, but evidently he was given a notice of some kind because he had time to grease the skids before he left.

*The manager said to himself, "What shall I do now? My master is taking away my job. I'm not strong enough to dig, and I'm ashamed to beg—I know what I'll do so that, when I lose my job here, people will welcome me into their houses.*

LUKE 16:3-4

With that he went to each of his master's two debtors and dramatically lowered their bills, one by 50 percent and one by 20 percent. Now here's the part that is hard to understand:

*The master commended the dishonest manager because he had acted shrewdly. For the people of this world are more shrewd in dealing with their own kind than are the people of the light. I tell you, use worldly wealth to gain friends for yourselves, so that when it is gone, you will be welcomed into eternal dwellings.*

LUKE 16:8-9

Remember who told this parable—Jesus Christ. Is He condoning dishonest behavior? That would be inconsistent with His other teachings as well as His nature. What, then, is the meaning of this strange parable?

Jesus catches our attention here to illustrate how important it is for us to be shrewd. His point to this parable is that we should see the wealth of this world as an opportunity to invest in eternity. Worldly wealth will not last; it will be gone someday, Jesus reminds us. Yet if we are shrewd, worldly money can be invested here and now for eternally good purposes.

That's why Jesus said,

*Do not store up for yourselves treasures on earth, where moth and rust destroy, and where thieves break in and steal. But store up for yourselves treasures in heaven, where moth and rust do not destroy, and where thieves do not break in and steal.*

MATTHEW 6:19-20

This shrewdness is personified in a manager who looked beyond the current mess he was in and prepared for his future. He had a long-term perspective, and it paid off!

## No Bed of His Own

Some time ago I returned home from a long business trip, in which I had spent nine days in nine cities, nine different hotels, nine different rooms, nine different beds. I was, as always, so glad to get back home. The plane just couldn't fly fast enough for me that night, the luggage couldn't come quickly enough, the taxi driver couldn't maneuver through traffic well enough to suit me. I was ready to be back in my own home, with my own things around me, and my own bed to sleep in.

I crawled into my warm bed with such a feeling of joy that night, and I got a wonderful night's sleep, so much better than I had in the hotel beds. I woke early the next morning, enjoying the luxury of no immediate deadline, and quietly thanked God for bringing me back safely home, to sleep in my own bed.

In those quiet moments, a verse of Scripture came to my mind about beds, found in Luke 9:58. Jesus and the disciples were walking along a road, with people following as usual, and one of those who had heard Jesus speak was obviously impressed with Him. He said to Jesus, "I will follow you wherever you go." Jesus replied: "Foxes have holes and birds of the air have nests, but the Son of Man has no place to lay his head."

As I lay in my snug, warm bed, for the first time I thought about the fact that during His earthly ministry Jesus never had a bed of His own. He never had His own place; He didn't own a home or condo, nor did He rent an apartment just for Himself. He didn't have His own space. He was always sleeping in someone else's bed. Oh, I'm certain He was warmly welcomed in many of those homes where He was given refuge, and undoubtedly many gave Him the best bed in the house while He was there. Yet none of these were His bed.

I then thought about the nine beds I had slept in over the previous week and a half. They were in nice hotels; I got service that I wouldn't even get at home: Clean sheets every night, meals in my room, someone else cleaning up after me. Yet I much preferred my own bed.

Then I thought about Jesus leaving what He had in heaven to come to earth, to bring me redemption. He was willing to be a servant; He was willing to live a nomadic life of ministry, going from one place to another, never having His own surroundings. In heaven He had been the center of all attention, and undoubtedly had lived in total luxury with nothing lacking. He had created space, and yet He relinquished all that and lived on this earth, with no space of His own, not even a bed.

Several things occurred to me as I thought about this. First, I realized anew how much my Savior did so that I could have life abundant. I appreciated His sacrifice even more, as I understood how much I would miss my bed, and knew that it wasn't any easier for Jesus to live without a place of His own than it would be for me.

Then I remembered the context of this verse. Jesus didn't say this in order to gain sympathy for Himself. He stated it as a fact to a man who had declared that he would follow Jesus everywhere and anywhere. I

suppose if someone came up to me and said, "Mary, I think you're ter-
rific, I believe in what you're doing, and I'm going to give up all of my
plans and follow you," I'd be flattered. I imagine I would encourage
him or her, thinking how great it would be to have someone doing
things for me.

Yet Jesus, of course, never responds like we would expect Him to.
In the face of this man's enthusiastic offer, Jesus explains very clearly
that to follow Him will mean a life of sacrifice, not a life of self-glory
and easy living. "In fact," Jesus says to him, "if you follow Me you may
not even have a bed of your own."

## The Cost of Discipleship

I snuggled deeper under the covers that morning as I pondered this
unusual response from Jesus, and I said, "Lord, what if You asked me
to give up my own bed for You, my own space? What would I do?"

I thought anew about the cost of discipleship. Jesus has never painted
rosy pictures of what it's like to be His person in this world. He has
always told it like it is, and He abruptly informed this man who
declared he wanted to be His disciple that there was a cost attached to
it: it would rearrange his priorities, change his ambitions, and turn his
life topsy-turvy; in fact, he might even have to give up his bed.

Now don't get me wrong. Certainly Christ offers many wonderful
things when we become His disciples: peace and joy, rest, abundant
life—and many more. Yet Jesus has always made it clear that it will be
on His terms, not ours, and His terms are that we lose our life in order
to find His life, that we die to ourselves in order to become alive unto
God.

On that cold morning in my own warm bed, I asked myself what

I had ever sacrificed in order to follow Jesus. It was a short list and not terribly impressive. Some income, undoubtedly; some opportunities at earthly success that had passed by; some companionships that might have been temporarily enjoyable; some time that I could have heaped on myself and "done my own thing." Yet it was a meagerly list, not worthy to be called sacrificial.

Of course, I also realized that what I had been given in exchange was immeasurably more than anything I could sacrifice, and so to become a disciple at any price is to make the best bargain you'll ever make. Whatever sacrifice you make no longer seems significant, because the return on the investment is beyond measure.

Yet I couldn't help asking myself if there was a cost of discipleship that I had not been willing to pay. Did I really understand what it meant to be a committed disciple of Jesus Christ? Could it be that He would even ask me to give up my own space, my own things, my comfortable surroundings, my familiar world—my own bed?

## Giving Back What Has Been Given to You

A couple of things happened then, in those quiet moments. I simply prayed, "Lord, I want to give You back what You've given to me and what I enjoy very much—my very own bed. Lord, it represents something important to me—my space and my right to have my own space, a right we hold dearly these days. It represents my roots, the place I can always come home to and feel comfortable. I don't think I ever truly realized how important it was to me until now, and I'd sure have some adjustments to make if I didn't have my own bed. But, I just want You to know, if that's literally what You ask of me, please make me willing to literally do it. And if it's not literal, please help me to keep ever mindful that everything I have is Yours, even my own space. And help me to remember that You gave up Your space to come to this earth for me."

Then I remembered the Scriptures that tell us that in this world we are aliens and strangers. The old song puts it so well: "This world is not my home, I'm just a-passing through...." We who are born from above are not at home in this world. We are simply sleeping in borrowed beds, just as I did on my business trip. It won't ever feel like home to us, because Jesus is not yet exalted as the King of kings and Lord of lords, and we can't be really comfortable in this foreign land.

Finally I remembered what Jesus told His disciples just before His crucifixion. He reminded them that He would be leaving, but urged them not to be despondent, because He was planning to come back and get them. In the meantime, guess what He's doing: He's getting our space ready for us in heaven.

It is a great comfort to realize that Jesus knows we have this need for our space, for a place where we are always welcome and a place that is comfortable for us—we need our own beds. So, in His ever-faithful manner, He is now getting that space ready for us. He said, "I go to prepare a place for you" (Jn 14:3b). Frankly, I choose to be simple and childlike enough to believe that literally. Jesus is decorating my room for me now in heaven, and someday I'll be home.

If I thought it was nice to crawl into my own earthly bed after the tiring trip and the nine hotel beds, just try to imagine what it's going to be like when we arrive home, really home, forever, never to leave again, in our own space, sharing it forever with all the saints, glorifying Jesus with all that we have.

God spoke to me in those quiet moments in my own bed that morning, and gave me some new insights and inspiration. I trust I'll never be the same for it. I pray I'll appreciate all the good things God has given me even more, and have a greater appreciation for the great sacrifice He made to come to earth for me. My desire is to hold everything given to me in loose, open hands, so that I'll always be willing to follow Him in obedience, whatever the cost.

I also want to stay focused on eternity, and not on this pilgrimage here. I'm just sleeping in a few hotel rooms here on this earth; sometimes they're pleasant, sometimes not. Yet no matter, really, because I'm not home yet. But I know I will be someday, and that homecoming will be greater than anything I've ever experienced or even imagined on this earth.

This is our great and marvelous hope, and these Forever Eyes will gives us freedom from being a slave to money and being possessed by our possessions.

**Nine**

# Looking at Marriage and Singleness With *Forever* Eyes

I make it a policy never to write or counsel on the topic of marriage. That's because I am single and my credentials are suspect when it comes to marriage, given that I've been divorced for thirty years! I've written a book on singleness (*Common Mistakes Singles Make,* published by Baker Books) that delves into the many issues of the single life for Christian adults.

So, why have I included a chapter in this book on marriage and singleness? Because all of you are either married or in some state of singleness, and our marriage state is of such significance in this earthly life that it surely can't be ignored in a discussion of eternal values.

## All Single in Eternity

We know from Scripture that there will be no marriage in eternity. We will all be single. The Sadducees tried to trap Jesus by asking him a hypothetical question about whose wife a woman would be at the resurrection, since she had been married to seven brothers. The Sadducees did not believe in the resurrection, so this was obviously a trick question, and they thought they had Jesus pinned against the wall. Yet notice how Jesus answered:

*You are in error because you do not know the Scriptures or the power of God. At the resurrection people will neither marry nor be given in marriage; they will be like the angels in heaven.*

MATTHEW 22:29-30

So, we won't have a married or single status in heaven. However, we will recognize each other in heaven, so you will know your marriage partner on the other side of eternity. Paul said, "Now I know in part; then I shall know fully, even as I am fully known" (1 Cor 13:12b). I think that must be great comfort for those whose mates have preceded them into eternity. We will know each other and enjoy renewed fellowship and companionship in eternity.

Those of us who are single have a tendency to see our lives as somewhat second-class, as though marriage is the norm and we are a bit subnormal. The Bible doesn't teach that, but society seems to send that message to us in various ways. Isn't it encouraging to realize that everyone will be single in heaven? We're getting in practice for eternity. Cool!

### Choose Your Mate Well

Marriage is a God-ordained covenant, and as such, should be highly honored and respected here on earth. God told us that it was good for us to have mates and companions, to meet our need for earthly intimacy and support. We need a very high view of marriage, its privileges, its responsibilities, and its vows. In a culture where 50 percent of marriages now end in divorce, it is easy to devalue its importance. It's easy to forget that God takes the marriage vows very seriously and expects us to as well.

Looking at marriage with Forever Eyes should cause us to be far more careful in choosing a life mate. I've written a book about eagles and the spiritual insights we can gain from them (*Soaring on High*, published by Moody Press), and we can learn a valuable lesson from the way the eagles choose their mates. Eagles mate for life, so it seems that this choice is not taken lightly or made emotionally. In fact, the female eagle will put her prospective suitor through a series of tests to see if he is qualified to be a good father. After all, if you are fully intent on mating for life, you can't afford to make a bad decision!

When you look with Forever Eyes at your choice of a mate, it should cause you to carefully consider the consequences of that choice in ten years, twenty years, fifty years! If you truly intend to stick with this partner, no matter what, you want to be sure he or she is God's choice for your life.

Of course, no one can predict the future, but we can look for the characteristics and traits that will make for a long and strong marriage. A woman needs to find a man who is both ready and willing to be the spiritual head of her home. You don't want to be begging him to go to church with you each week, or waiting for him to initiate family devotions. You want a man who desires that as much or more than you do!

Does he initiate prayer and Bible study with you during your courting time? Does he voluntarily talk of things of God, study his Bible, get involved in God's work? If not, do you think he will just automatically change once you marry him?

A man needs to look for a woman who has a gentle and quiet spirit, as Peter mentions in 1 Peter 3:4. However, let me hasten to add that shouldn't mean she is a wallflower. A gentle and quiet spirit can reside in a woman who is gregarious, outgoing, even assertive. (I speak from experience!) Nonetheless, you want a woman whose inward beauty is even greater than her outward beauty. I know that looks and shape and form are important to your male eyes, and that's OK. Yet don't let that cause you to overlook the inward beauty of a woman, which, believe me, will be far more important and lasting in the long run. Look at her with Forever Eyes—how God sees her—and you will make a much better decision about your mate for life.

### Singleness Through Earthly Eyes

Perhaps a greater challenge is for us who are still single here on this earth. Given our natural desires to be married and have a family, singleness can sometimes seem like a prison or a punishment. To look at singleness with Forever Eyes is very difficult for some of us to do.

Again, I speak from experience. I became a single working mom when my daughter was eight years old. This certainly was never part of my life's plan, but it happened. I then began a ten-year roller-coaster ride of trying my best to get married again. I thought that to be single was a curse; I thought happiness could never really be mine unless I was married; I thought I would be incomplete until I married again. So, I determined to find a man!

For the first ten years of my single-again life, I looked at singleness through my earthly eyes. I refused to let God give me an eternal view. I didn't want anyone telling me that I could find fulfillment in singleness. I was certain that I knew what was best for me, and that was marriage, nothing else.

This reminds me of a letter I received from a single woman who asked for advice and encouragement. She said she wanted to be married and was very depressed and discouraged because God hadn't given her a husband. She told me in her letter, "Don't tell me that God is my husband and Jesus can fulfill all my needs; I want a real husband."

A few years earlier, I could have been that woman, saying those same words. I had to write her back what must have seemed like a very discouraging letter, because the only answer I can ever give is the one she told me not to give her. I gently reminded her that God does not owe her anything, not even a husband. She owes—and you and I owe—God everything.

When you look at your singleness with earthly eyes, it can lead you to desperateness, to anger with God, to despair, to wrong choices, to sinful lifestyles, and to settling for less than God's best. This, then, becomes self-inflicted suffering. When you choose to see your singleness as a burden, you have chosen a life of dissatisfaction, restlessness, and misery.

### Singleness Through Forever Eyes

Looking at singleness with Forever Eyes may not be easy, but it's easier than the other way! Paul wrote in 1 Corinthians 7:25-28,

> Now about virgins: I have no command from the Lord, but I *give a judgment as one who by the Lord's mercy is trustworthy. Because of the present crisis, I think that it is good for you to remain as you are. Are you married? Do not seek a divorce. Are you unmarried? Do not look for a wife. But if you do marry, you have not sinned; and if a virgin marries, she has not sinned. But those who marry will face many troubles in this life, and I want to spare you this.*

I doubt you've heard many messages on this passage, but there it is, in God's Word. And we know that "All Scripture is God-breathed and is useful for teaching, rebuking, correcting and training in righteousness" (2 Tm 3:16). Paul couldn't have said it much more clearly: "Those who marry will face many troubles in this life."

Marriage is hard; it takes lots of effort to make it work. Yes, when it is of God, it certainly brings many wonderful benefits. Yet the grass on that side of the fence is not always green.

In speaking to some single women recently, I was answering a question about the role of women in a godly relationship, and what God expects from us. Does the "submission" issue begin in the courting relationship, or only after the marriage vows are taken?

I reminded these young women that relationships are never easy. A good relationship—especially with someone as close as a mate—requires lots of dying to self. It is a never-ending challenge to put the other person first, to adjust to that person, and that means there will be lots of give and take.

I have a friend who married in her late thirties. She did so only after a great amount of consultation and counseling with godly people. She was not desperate; she wanted to make certain this was a God thing. Yet even at that, when I spoke to her a few months after the wedding, she said, "Mary, I didn't know what a bad person I was until I got married." I could understand what she meant, for marriage at its best is a process of continual adjustment to the needs and desires of one's mate. The selfishness and stubbornness that may be buried deep inside come to the surface once the two become one.

Yes, marriage offers many wonderful benefits, and I'm not trying to negate those. I only want those of you who are single to look at marriage with God's eyes and see it in its cold, hard reality, instead of through Hollywood eyes or from an idealistic viewpoint.

## Marriage Through Forever Eyes

For those who are married, my words will be brief, since I'm single. I have learned much about marriage through my friendships with some wonderful couples. When you look at your marriage with God's Forever Eyes, you are taking very seriously those vows, "'til death do us part." I would imagine that almost every married couple goes through at least one period when one or both of them thinks seriously about calling it quits. There are many good reasons to abandon those vows and just give up.

I think of several couples that I personally know who have faced those days. Sometimes you look for someone to sympathize with you and encourage you to follow through and walk out. The romance is gone, the good feelings are gone, and the desire to try again is gone. That's when you desperately need Forever Eyes.

Look at your choices with Forever Eyes. What will matter in eternity? What is the best choice for your children, who are eternal?

Of course, there are situations where separation is the right thing to do, in cases of abuse or abandonment, for example. One woman recently wrote to tell me that she had stayed with her husband for over thirty years, raised their four children, supported the family financially, carried all the responsibilities, because her husband just refused to be accountable or dependable in any area of their lives. She was asking me if it was not now time for her to begin a life of her own, since she had truly been on her own through most of the marriage. This kind of situation may indeed qualify as a just reason for separation, after many years of going the extra mile and truly taking one's vows very seriously.

Yet cases like this are the exception and not the rule. Through Forever Eyes, marriage vows are of great importance, and preserving the marriage if at all possible should be our earnest goal.

## Either Way, Use Forever Eyes

So whether married or single, your challenge is to look with Forever Eyes at your situation. If you are learning to number your days, as we discussed in chapter 7, you can again ask yourself, "What difference will it make in eternity?" Neither marriage nor singleness will give us any advantage in heaven. Yet how we handle our single or married status here on earth will matter, because it will demonstrate our trust—or lack of trust—in God.

The person who marries the wrong mate just to avoid being single will never realize his or her full potential for Jesus Christ. That poor choice will affect this person's ability to do the good works God prepared in advance for him or her to do, as we are told in Ephesians 2:10.

Furthermore, the married person who treats his or her marriage vows with disrespect and easily gives up on that marriage is equally in danger of missing God's best. Imagine being confronted with your marriage vows and trying to explain to Jesus at the Judgment Seat that you just weren't "fulfilled," you just weren't "in love" any longer, or your mate no longer "met your needs." I dare say those excuses, which are common here on earth, will hold no water in heaven.

Whether married or single, separated, divorced, or widowed—in whatever state you find yourself at this time—ask God to help you see it with Forever Eyes. Even if you think it is impossible to change your attitude toward your singleness or your marriage, give God permission to do it if He can. Remember, whether you are single or married for the few short years that remain to you here on earth will have little significance in heaven. Yet your faithfulness to God's Word will matter greatly.

## Ten

# What Blots Out *E*ternity?

A saint of old, Amos Wells, wrote: "Heal me of my blindness that blots out eternity with this bit of mortal life close pressed." His old English words make us read this sentence more than once to grasp its meaning. When we do, we recognize the importance of this simple prayer.

We need to be healed of the blindness that prevents us from seeing the unseen, from looking with Forever Eyes. I wrote his prayer in my journal several years ago and have often repeated it to the Lord.

### Mortal Versus Immortal

This "bit of mortal life" is a good reminder that the things that blot out eternity from our view are mortal, not immortal. This means that they don't last very long. Furthermore, they are bits—small and inconsequential compared to the unseen things of eternity. Yet because this mortal life is close pressed, right in front of our eyes all the time, it frequently keeps us from looking with Forever Eyes.

There could be a scene of unsurpassed beauty and grandeur in front of you, but if you hold a worthless piece of play money up close to your eyes, it will keep you from seeing the magnificent scene behind it. It will blot out the beautiful with the worthless. How often we allow useless, worthless, meaningless, mortal things to blot out the everlasting view God has for us, waiting there to be seen with Forever Eyes.

I've been a single working mom since my daughter was in grade school. I began a career with IBM in sales and worked hard to succeed. After four years I was offered a headquarters position in training for our sales organization. This job required considerable travel.

I looked at this through my everyday eyes and saw the money this position would bring, the prestige of getting a promotion, and the perceived excitement of traveling worldwide as a "competitive expert" in the company, and made a decision to take the job.

Had I looked at this opportunity with Forever Eyes, I would have seen the weeks I would spend away from my daughter, the instability this would bring into her life, the loneliness she would encounter, the feelings of abandonment she would have. One look through Forever Eyes would have definitely caused me to make a different decision and choose what was eternally important—my daughter's welfare. This "bit of mortal life" pressed close in around my eyes, however, and it blinded me to eternity.

### Loving the World

The "mortal life" to which Wells refers is called the "world" in Scripture:

> *Do not love the world or anything in the world. If anyone loves the world, the love of the Father is not in him. For everything in the world—the cravings of sinful man, the lust of his eyes and the boasting of what he has and does—comes not from the Father but from the world. The world and its desires pass away, but the man who does the will of God lives forever.*

> 1 JOHN 2:15-17

"World" here does not refer to God's creation, but to the world system, which includes our own sinful cravings, our lustful eyes, and our arrogant pride. We all have the world in us. The Bible teaches that we were born with a sinful nature, so this trilogy of the lust of the flesh, the lust of the eyes, and the pride of life, as the King James Version translates it, is ready to run rampant in each of our hearts. It is one of these, or some combination thereof, that "blots out eternity."

### The Appetite of the Eyes

"Feast your eyes on this" is a cliché we have all used. Your eyes have an appetite. They want something satisfying. Left to themselves, they want the things the world system offers. They lust for what they see when looking through earthbound eyes.

This eye lust that inflicts all of us is not very discriminating or discerning. We are often quite willing to settle for less, for the seen things, rather than seeing the unseen things that are of eternal value. Our desires may be legitimate, but we try to satisfy them with the seen world, with less than the best, or, sadder still, with evil substitutes. This "bit of mortal life" will lead us to satisfy normal desires in forbidden ways.

Mind you, we don't do this knowingly. In our deception, we attempt to satisfy our desires with what looks very satisfying. The seen world often presents us with a beautiful façade, drawing us into its web, where we discover that it can't fulfill its promise.

What causes this blindness to the unseen world that blots out eternity? We are looking through earthly eyes instead of Forever Eyes. We are not intentional about seeing through Forever Eyes, or we don't know how, or we forget how, or we choose the lustful eyes of this world instead.

## The Power of Eyesight

Vision is our most powerful sense. Information and impressions enter our minds through the avenues of verbal communication (our choice of words), vocal communication (our tone of voice), and nonverbal communication (what we see). In a typical interaction, verbal communication has a 7 percent impact, vocal communication has a 38 percent impact, and nonverbal communication has a 55 percent impact on what we know, how we respond, and what we feel. The impact of the nonverbal component of communication is larger than that of the other two combined.

Jesus said, "The eye is the lamp of the body. If your eyes are good, your whole body will be full of light. But if your eyes are bad, your whole body will be full of darkness. If then the light within you is darkness, how great is that darkness!" (Mt 6:22-23). He reminds us that through the eye the body finds its way, because light enters through the eye. Good eyes let in lots of light, so that we can find our way. Bad eyes let in no light, so darkness descends and keeps us from finding our way. This is a pretty simple concept, with eternal ramifications.

In his book *The Holy War*, John Bunyan depicts the war of the believer against our enemy, Satan. In this allegory, Mansoul, representing a person, is a town beseiged by the enemy, Diabolus. One of the enemy's chief avenues of entrance into this town is Eye-Gate.

That's a very accurate way to think about our visual sense. It is the gateway to our souls, to our hearts, to our emotions, to our attitudes. What we feast our eyes on is largely responsible for who we are.

## Obstructions to Forever Eyes

As humans we have certain cravings that are common to us all. We crave significance, love, intimacy, and meaning for our inner selves. We crave food and physical necessities for our outer selves. These cravings are not sinful in themselves. Yet they can easily lead us down wrong paths into that lust of the flesh, lust of the eyes, and pride of life that John calls the world.

Lust is defined as a passionate or overmastering desire. When normal cravings become domineering and begin to control us, we have moved into the "lust zone." Our culture today is most complicit in aiding and abetting our lusts. It bombards our eyes with images that stir up a desire to meet normal cravings in forbidden ways.

To illustrate some things that blot out eternity for us, let's consider what happens in our daily routines that can serve to obstruct our view of eternity.

### Television/Movies/Videos

No generation has been so subjected to the ready availability of visual trash as this present one. I'm certain I don't have to list the many eye-gates that are in our homes through television and videos, as well as in movie theaters.

In a recent sermon on our entertainment industry, my pastor, Dr. Erwin Lutzer of Moody Memorial Church in Chicago, challenged us to carefully watch what we watch! He gave us three tests for discerning whether to watch something or not—for determining if it will "blot out eternity" and prevent Forever Eyes. I pass them on to you because they were meaningful to me:

1. Check out the content. One easy test is to ask yourself, "Would I

look at this if Jesus were sitting right here beside me?" Then, of course, you should remind yourself that His Spirit is indeed right there with you, and what you watch, He watches. Often we laugh at what grieves the heart of God.

2. Check out its control over you. Could you stop watching this at any time, or have you become addicted to it?

3. Check out the amount of time it takes from you. Paul wrote, "See then that ye walk circumspectly, not as fools, but as wise, redeeming the time, because the days are evil" (Eph 5:15-16, KJV). When we redeem something, we buy it back, and we can buy back from this mortal life the time we spend looking at temporary things by investing that same time in eternal things.

I sailed through points one and two of his sermon without a twinge of conscience, for I have learned to screen out the junk and degradation that fills our airwaves. Yet when he got to number three, he went from "preachin' to meddlin'," and I began to wonder what my life would be like if I spent my viewing time reading good books or listening to good music or something like that. How often have I blotted out eternity with some bit of mortal-life viewing that, though innocent, was a poor use of time?

I wish I had learned much earlier in my life what I'm coming to learn now, and that is that doing it God's way is the easy way. Not only is it right, but in the end, it is easier. Oh, it takes some discipline up front that may come hard for me, but the results are imminently more beneficial to me. I remove large amounts of struggle, difficulty, pain, and hardship from my life, both now and in the future, when I simply go God's way.

Therefore, when I am willing to remove any obstacle that "blots out eternity" from my eyesight, so that I can see through Forever Eyes, I enrich my life a hundredfold. With that kind of return on my investment, why do I ever allow bits of this mortal life to blot out eternity, when I can at any time remove those obstacles and look through Forever Eyes? Any reasonably intelligent person should be able to see the logic of this truth.

### Success/Money/Status

These three things seem to go hand in hand in our culture today; you can't have one—or two—without the other. The pursuit of these bits of mortal life can blind us perhaps quicker than anything else.

I am privileged to serve on the Board of Trustees of LeTourneau University in Longview, Texas, a university devoted to high academic standards and strong Bible teaching. The chaplain told me of one of their recent graduates who had been offered a phenomenal six-figure starting salary with a Fortune 10 computer software company. I was staggered at the figure, but was even more amazed that the young man had turned the job down and chosen a position with a lesser-known company at a much lower salary. His reason for turning down the big bucks: "It's not where God wanted me to be," he said.

How marvelous and unusual to see one so young who is already proficient at looking with Forever Eyes. I pray he will continue to avoid the blindness that blots out eternity, for if he does, his potential in God's kingdom is awesome. And the big bucks he has turned down here will be compensated for by the huge eternal investment his life will make and send on ahead of him to heaven.

Jesus warned us again and again about the power of money and all that goes with it. The lust for money brings a blindness from which few are ever healed.

Agur gave us a wise saying, found in Proverbs 30:8-9: "Keep false-hood and lies far from me; give me neither poverty nor riches, but give me only my daily bread. Otherwise, I may have too much and disown you and say, 'Who is the Lord?' Or I may become poor and steal, and so dishonor the name of my God."

## Busyness/Misplaced Priorities/Endless Activity

Years ago I began to pray that God would deliver me from being addicted to activity. That prayer came as a result of my own tendency to blot out eternity—what really matters—with a very busy schedule. Mind you, most of that schedule was focused on ministry of some sort. Yet even so, given my personality, I could blot out an eternal perspective in my daily life by becoming so busy that there was no time to use my Forever Eyes. Each day became a contest to see if I could make it through my to-do list for the day.

It came as a shock to me when I realized that I took great pride in my busyness, my endless activities. I loved to talk about how busy I was. I enjoyed the admiration I would get from others because I was so busy. It was the pride-of-life worldliness that John identified as part of this world system, and it subtly blotted out eternity. How seductive and deceptive it was—and can still be.

Now I find myself very uncomfortable when anyone starts to comment about "how busy I am." That's not how I want to be known. It can become an excuse for not focusing on eternal matters, or as I often found true in my case, for doing eternally important activities without an eternal focus.

For example, it is possible to be involved in a ministry that is part of God's kingdom work without ever thinking about its eternal significance. When I lose that eternal focus, my motivation turns sour. The ministry goes from God-centered to me-centered, and soon it becomes a drudgery or a job rather than a joy at being part of something eternally important.

## What Blots Out Eternity for You?

I've illustrated just a few of the things that blot out eternity for many of us. Your list could be different. And keep in mind, it could be a good thing, not necessarily an evil thing.

An eternal eye exam might be a good exercise for all of us. If we are serious about living now in the light of eternity and investing the days that are left to us in God's heavenly assets, we must get rid of everything, big or small, that blots out eternity for us.

## Forever Eyes—A Daily Choice

Life is so daily—have you noticed? The will of God is lived out one day at a time. Therefore, if you and I are ever to live now in the light of eternity, we must begin today and continue on a daily basis. That simply means that we must be intentional about doing it. For me that means finding ways to remind myself that I have a choice at every turn in my day whether to see every person, every circumstance, every opportunity, every temptation through my earthly eyes, or instead to put on those Forever Eyes. This is our choice, and we have no one to blame but ourselves if we fail to do it.

I close this book with Paul's exhortation to Titus, which sums it up far better than I could:

*For the grace of God that brings salvation has appeared to all men. It teaches us to say "No" to ungodliness and worldly passions, and to live self-controlled, upright and godly lives in this present age, while we wait for the blessed hope—the glorious appearing of our great God and Savior, Jesus Christ, who gave himself for us to redeem us from all wickedness and to purify for himself a people that are his very own, eager to do what is good.*

TITUS 2:11-14

# Notes

Two
*Looking at Myself and My Past With Forever Eyes*

1. J.I. Packer, *Knowing God* (Downers Grove, Ill.: InterVarsity, 1973), 37.
2. Philip Yancey, *Reaching for the Invisible God* (Grand Rapids, Mich.: Zondervan, 2000), 165.

Four
*Looking at Desires With Forever Eyes*

1. John Ballie, *A Diary of Private Prayer* (New York: A Fireside Book published by Simon and Schuster, 1996), 91.

Six
*Looking at Difficulties With Forever Eyes*

1. John Piper, *The Hidden Smile of God* (Wheaton, Ill.: Crossway, 2001), 166.
2. Piper, 170.

Eight
*Looking at Money and Possessions With Forever Eyes*

1. Richard Foster, *The Challenge of the Disciplined Life: Christian Reflections on Money, Sex, and Power* (San Fransisco: Harper Collins, 1985), 26, 28.
2. Foster, 61.